A History of Dearborn County, Indiana

Aurora, Lawrenceburg, Greendale and Other Towns

Home School and History Buff Tourism Guide Series

Paul R. Wonning

A History of Dearborn County, Indiana
Published By Paul R. Wonning

mossyfeetbooks@gmail.com

If you would like email notification of when new Mossy Feet books become available email the author for inclusion in the subscription list.

Mossy Feet Books
www.mossyfeetbooks.com

Indiana Places

http://indianaplaces.blogspot.com/

Description

A History of Dearborn County serves as a great historical resource for home school students and Indiana history buffs. It includes information on museums, historical markers, National Register of Historic Sites and other areas of historical interest in Dearborn County, Indiana. The guide is a great help in planning field trips as local parks and nature preserves are included in the book, as well. Readers will discover historical information on Dearborn County cities and towns like Aurora, Lawrenceburg, Greendale the smaller communities in the county. Home schooling parents and local history buffs can use the book as a guide to finding Dearborn County's historical treasure for fun and educational field trips.

Table of Contents

A History of Dearborn County, Indiana
Paul R. Wonning

County History

The county form of local organization originated in England. The English counties, called shires, came into being as local units of government organization in the Ninth Century. The word "shire" derives from the Old High German word "scira" and means "care" or "official charge". A shire is a unit of local government control with a sheriff, appointed by the king, as the principal executive authority. The word "county" originated from the Old French word, "conté" which denoted a governmental division under the sovereignty of a count, or viscount. When the Normans of France conquered England in 1066 they brought the word with them. County and shire have become synonymous. When the English began colonizing North America they began organizing shires, or counties, as they spread inland. In the United States, and Canada, the county evolved as a local unit of government that originally used geographic features, such as creeks and rivers, as boundaries. These units typically have local officials, such as sheriffs and trustees, to govern them. Each county is subdivided into smaller divisions known as townships.

Counties in Indiana

Indiana has 92 counties, each with its own county seat, or capital, and governing local officials. The first county organized in what is now Indiana was Knox County, established when Indiana was still part of the Northwest Territory. Knox County, organized on June 20, 1790, included the current states, or parts of, Indiana, Michigan, Illinois, and Ohio. The last county organized in Indiana was Newton County, created by the state legislature on

December 8, 1859. The oldest counties, in general, are in the southern part of the state along the Ohio River and were separated from either the original Knox County or other later counties. Most of Indiana's counties were named after United States Founding Fathers, Revolutionary War heroes or men instrumental to Indiana's history. Most have little or no connection to the county whose name they bear.

County Seat

In general, county seats, the seat of a county's government, are located near the geographic center of the county. The county court house is located in the county seat. During the early phase of the state's history various towns within a county competed fiercely for the county seat. The seat, as the center of county government, attracted settlers in greater numbers and all citizens in the county had to visit the county seat periodically to pay taxes, obtain marriage licenses, land deeds and other official tasks. Thus, businesses located in county seats had more traffic than businesses in outlying towns. Property values were usually higher and there was higher prestige in having the county seat located in a particular town. Many county seats have been moved at least once and sometimes several times. These moves sometimes created conflicts, both legal, and physical, over the relocation. Shots have been fired over relocations and more than one time county records had to be moved secretly in the middle of the night to stave off conflicts.

Here is an alphabetical list of Indiana counties:

Adams

Allen

Bartholomew

Benton

Blackford

Boone

Brown

Carroll

Cass

Clark

Clay

Clinton

Crawford

Daviess

Dearborn

Decatur

De Kalb

Delaware

Dubois

Elkhart

Fayette

Floyd

Fountain

Franklin

Fulton

Gibson

Grant

Greene

Hamilton

Hancock

Harrison

Hendricks

Henry

Howard

Huntington

Jackson

Jasper

Jay

Jefferson

Jennings

Johnson

Knox

Kosciusko

La Porte

Lagrange

Lake

Lawrence

Madison

Marion

Marshall

Martin

Miami

Monroe

Montgomery

Morgan

Newton

Noble

Ohio

Orange

Owen

Parke

Perry

Pike

Porter

Posey

Pulaski

Putnam

Randolph

Ripley

Rush

St. Joseph

Scott

Shelby

Spencer

Starke

Steuben

Sullivan

Switzerland

Tippecanoe

Tipton

Union

Vanderburgh

Vermillion

Vigo

Wabash

Warren

Warrick

Washington

Wayne

Wells

White

Whitley

Power of Indiana Counties

The United States Constitution leaves the organization and function of county government to the individual states, thus organization and powers of county government can vary from state to state. Article 6, Section 2 of the Indiana Constitution establishes specific county offices. Article 6, Section 3 allows the General Assembly to create new offices for counties and townships as it sees fit. Article 6, Section 8 the Constitution gives the General Assembly the power of impeachment of county officials and the mechanism to fill county official vacancies that may occur after the General Election. Article 9, Section 3 gives the counties the power to create farms to care for individuals that, due to age, infirmity or misfortune to care for these individuals and see to their welfare. In general, counties have powers to legislate as long as the proposed statute is not expressly forbidden by the state constitution or not within the state's jurisdiction. Legislative powers of counties can be confusing and a further discussion of their powers is beyond the author's scope of understanding. If the reader has further questions about the county's powers, it is best to consult with an attorney.

Local Government Organization in Indiana

Local governments within counties in Indiana consist of townships and incorporated towns and cities.

Townships

Townships are smaller governing units within a county. A Township Trustee, elected by voters within their township, represents those voters in the township, which also elects a three-member Township Board to assist the Trustee.

Incorporated Towns and Cities

Incorporated towns and cities elect their own representatives independent of the township. These officials include the mayor and the city or town council. Depending upon the organization of the local government, there may be other elected officials.

Constitutionally Created County Officials

Sheriff

Clerk of Circuit Court

Auditor

Recorder

Coroner

Treasurer

Surveyor

Prosecuting Attorney

The prosecutor represents the State of Indiana in all court cases in the district to which they are elected.

County Officials Created by the Assembly

Judge

County Council

Board of County Commissioners

County Assessor

Some Counties have:

Superior Court

County Court

Sheriff

The sheriff has both county and state functions. The sheriff administers the county jail and is responsible for prisoners held within the jail. The sheriff administers work release programs. The sheriff collects delinquent taxes for both the county and the Indiana Department of Revenue. The sheriff is authorized to appoint deputies as approved by the county commissioners. Most times the county 911 emergency response system is maintained by the sheriff's department. The sheriff's department is the primary law enforcement agency within a county. The sheriff and their deputies have jurisdiction everywhere within their county, including all towns and cities. In Indiana a sheriff is elected to a four year term and is limited to two terms. According to Indiana Code 36-2-13-5, the sheriff's duties include:

Arrest persons who commit an offense within the Sheriff's jurisdiction

Suppress breaches of the peace

Calling the power of the county to the Sheriff's aid if necessary

Pursue and jail felons

Serve or execute all process directed to the Sheriff by legal authority

Attend and preserve order in all courts of the county

Operate the county jail and care for the prisoners therein.

Indiana law additionally specifies that the Sheriff maintain records, facilitate the sex offender registry within the county, serve state tax warrants, conduct Sheriff Sales on foreclosed homes, and issue handgun permits. In Elkhart County, when someone calls 911 or needs help, particularly outside the municipal limits, the Sheriff gets the calls.

Clerk of Circuit Court

The clerk is the guardian of democratic government in Indiana. It is the clerk's responsibility to execute a smooth election process in the county. The clerk must administer Indiana's elections in a fair manner. The clerk also receives candidate filings and certifies election results. The Clerk appoints members to the county election board and is a member of that board. It is up to the clerk to assure that all polling places in the county are in compliance with Indiana's laws.

In addition to this, the clerk maintains all of the county's court records and issues marriage licenses and draws the names of prospective jurors for court cases. The clerk also collects fines, court cost payments and money judgments from civil cases. The clerk pays this money out to the person or entity entitled to the judgment. Child support payments are also the responsibility of the clerk.

Auditor

The auditor maintains the county's financial accounts and issues checks. The auditor works closely with the county commissioners in budgetary matters. The auditor also serves as the secretary for the board of county commissioners and as clerk to the county council. The auditor takes the taxes collected by the Treasurer and distributes it to the county agencies. As the principal financial officer of the county, the auditor must also develop financial analysis and cash flow projections. The auditor must also prepare an annual report so the commissioners can develop a budget.

Recorder

The recorder maintains the county's records. The records include property deeds, marriages, mortgages, liens, military discharges, leases and powers of attorney.

Coroner

The coroner's function is to determine the cause of death in instances of death caused by violence, accident or death under suspicious circumstances. The coroner is to employ a qualified pathologist to perform an autopsy if one is needed. The coroner must then file a death certificate with the local health officer.

Treasurer

The county treasurer is responsible for collecting all taxes due to the county from individuals, the state and other sources. The treasurer works with the auditor to ensure that county monies are distributed properly.

Surveyor

The county surveyor's duties include preparing, maintaining and making available to the public section maps, grants, subdivisions and other property parcel records in the county.

Prosecuting Attorney

The Prosecuting Attorney bears responsibility for enforcing Indiana's laws within the county. They also prosecute felony and misdemeanor crimes in the county, appoint grand juries and conduct investigations into crimes. They also have the power to prosecute minor crimes like traffic violations, juvenile cases and other infractions.

Judge

The county judicial system lies at the center of Indiana's judicial system. A county's voters elect the county judge, whose term is for six years. The governor has the power to appoint a county judge when a vacancy occurs between elections. Judges preside over civil and criminal cases within a county as well as other judicial functions. The county circuit court serves as the court of original jurisdiction for cases in a county. For a more detailed explanation of the functions of a county court, consult an attorney.

Some Counties have:

Superior Court

County Court

Board of County Commissioners

Indiana Statute requires that county commissioners meet monthly. They may meet oftener, if need arises. The county auditor acts as the clerk of the board of commissioners and must keep records of all proceedings in the Auditor's office.

County Council

Each county is divided into districts of varying number. Generally, a council member is elected from each district, with three at-large members. The council is a body created by the General Assembly is not a constitutionally created position. The County Council has the ultimate power over the county's fiscal matters. The council establishes the county budget, determines county employee pay scales and benefits, establishes the tax rates and authorizes all county expenditures and purchases. In general, Indiana code gives the following powers to the members of the county council:

Approving and fixing annual operating budgets of all county government offices and agencies. (IC 36-2-5-11)

Establishing salaries, wages, per diems and other compensation for all county officials and employees (IC 36-2-5-11)

Fixing tax rates and establishing levies on all county property for the purpose of raising funds to meet budget requirements in conducting county business, as well as authorizing the borrowing of money in the form of bonds and notes. (IC36-2-6-18)

Appropriating public funds, i.e., authorizing the expenditure of county money by particular officials or departments for specific purposes

Authorizing certain purchases or sales of county owned land (IC 36-1-11-3) or other real property (36-2-2-20)

County Assessor

The assessor uses the tax rates established by the county commissioners to assess property values in the county for taxation purposes. The assessor certifies those values to the auditor. Taxpayers may appeal the assessor's valuation of their property.

County Finances

County Sources of Revenue

Property Taxes

Income Taxes

State Funding

Federal Funding

Investment Income

Debt Funding

Miscellaneous Revenue

Property Taxes

All property within a county is subject to property tax, unless the property has been specifically declared exempt. The county assessor is responsible for setting property values, based upon rates set by the County Commissioners. Property tax valuation is a complicated procedure. For more information, contact your county assessor or commissioner.

Income Taxes

The State of Indiana permits counties to collect income taxes. These taxes are collected as a part of withholding with the Indiana Department of Revenue collecting them and distributing the revenue to the county. The county has multiple options for imposing this tax.

State Funding

The state distributes revenue collected from various taxes collected at the state level. These include aircraft, boat and taxes on financial institutions. This is not an all inclusive list, as the list also includes funds from inheritance taxes, alcoholic beverage fees and many other taxes and fees.

Federal Funding

The federal government also provides funding in the form of grants and other financial bequests.

Investment Income

Counties and localities are permitted to invest in certain Federal investments like Treasury bonds and the like. The interest collected on these investments can provide addition county funding.

Debt Funding

County and local governments are permitted to borrow money for specific projects. This can include short term loans, long term loans, bond issues and other forms of borrowing.

Miscellaneous Revenue

The State permits counties to impose several different types of special taxes, including motor vehicle excise surtaxes, innkeeper taxes, food and beverage taxes and "special benefit" taxes.

Note:

It is beyond the scope of this work to go into the complex system of county and local taxation. The author's intent is only to provide a general outline of a county's sources of revenue for informational purposes. For more information, contact your county commissioner or trustee.

Meetings and Records

The Indiana Constitution provides that county officials meet periodically and requires public notices of such meetings and that records be kept of the proceedings.

Dearborn County

Basic County Information

County Seat – Lawrenceburg

Area - 307.42 square miles

Population - 49,331 (2016 estimate)

Founded - March 7, 1803

Named for- Dr. Henry Dearborn

County Government

Administration Offices

165 Mary St

Lawrenceburg, IN 47025

(812) 537-1040

https://www.dearborncounty.org

Tourism Information

Dearborn County Visitor Center

320 Walnut Street

Lawrenceburg, IN 47025

812-537-0814

800-322-8198

dearborn@visitsoutheastindiana.com

https://www.visitsoutheastindiana.com

Dearborn County Climate and Weather

Rainfall (in.) - 42.4739 - 39.2

Snowfall (in.) - 16.7666 - 25.8

Precipitation Days - 79.5 - 102

Sunny Days – 179.205

Avg. July High - 86.722   86.1

Avg. Jan. Low - 22.422 - 22.6

Comfort Index (higher=better) - 49   54

UV Index - 3.6 - 4.3

Elevation ft. - 790 -1,443

USDA Zone 5b -15°F to -10°F

USDA Zone 6a -10°F to -5°F

USDA Zone 6b -5°F to 0°F

USDA Zone 7a 0°F to 5°F

The areas closest to the Ohio River are moderated by the river and are in USDA Zone 7a. The areas further north and west gradually grow colder in winter.

Dearborn County Geography:

The highest point in Dearborn County is in the northwestern part of the county near the town of Jackson, 1040 feet. The lowest elevation is the point where Laughery Creek drains into the Ohio River, 449 feet in the southeastern portion of the county. About 70 percent of Dearborn County is farmland. Farm products include livestock, corn, soybeans, chickens, tobacco and horses. Hay is also an important crop. The county also has some peach and apple orchards. The Whitewater River drains the eastern portion of the county, Laughery Creek the southern portion with Tanner and

Hogan Creeks draining the central and east central regions of the county. The Ohio River forms the southeastern border, with all the creeks and rivers draining into it. Broad upland plains form the topography of the north eastern, central and western portions of the county. Creeks have carved deep valleys into the terrain as they approach the Ohio River. Many of the valleys are prone to flooding during periods of high rainfall. A levee protects Lawrenceburg from flooding, however, Aurora is subject to periodic flooding from the Ohio River. Much of the water supply for the cities comes from deep wells dug in the gravelly areas near the river. Many residents in rural areas rely on dug wells or cisterns.

Position in the World

The Ohio River forms a portion of the southeast boundary between Dearborn County and Northern Kentucky. Laughery Creek provides the boundary between Dearborn and Ohio Counties, also on the southeast. Ripley County lies to immediate west and Franklin County to the north. The eastern boundary is the state line with Ohio lying to the east.

Thumbnail History

1798 - Israel Ludlow Surveys True Meridian That Became Indiana/Ohio State Line

By October 1798 Ludlow had completed surveying the Greenville Treaty line and was ready to begin surveying the Symmes tract in the region of the Great Miami River. Before he could begin surveying this, he needed to have a true north/south meridian from which he could base the remainder of the survey. The Northwest Territory Act had mandated that 5, and not more than 7, states be created from the vast territory. It had stated that the border between an "eastern state," and a "middle," state consist of a true meridian that proceeded due north from a point where the

Great Miami River enters the Ohio River. thus, Ludlow began surveying the true meridian that would become the line between the new Indiana Territory and the old Northwest Territory in 1800. In 1803 Ohio would become a state. The meridian survives today as the border between Ohio and Indiana.

Early Settlement

The first reported settlers began filtering into what is now Dearborn County along the Ohio River in 1794. Local lore suggests George Groves built the first log cabin on the banks of Laughery Creek. Another early settler, Nicholas Cheek, settled along Wilson Creek. Other accounts hold that Adam Flade was the first settler on land along South Hogan Creek in January 1796. Revolutionary War Veteran Ephraim Morrison followed, building the first log cabin and clearing the first trees along Hogan Creek somewhere in present day Aurora. Other settlers followed these first pioneers. These first settlers were squatters who did not have clear title to the land they occupied.

April 06, 1801 - Land Office in Cincinnati Began Selling Land

Already Settled

Settlers had already "squatted," on much of the land that was now on the market. The Whitewater and Laughery Creek valleys already contained cabins, farms and small settlements. The people that lived on these tracts did not own title to the lands, rather they possibly hoped to purchase their selections when the land office opened. Nonetheless, when the land office opened in Cincinnati people did not flock to the land office. The first purchases in what is now Dearborn County did not occur until April 9.

The opening of the land office gave people their first chance at purchasing the lands in southeastern Indiana. Joseph

Hayes made the first recorded land purchase in Dearborn County on April 9, 1801. Many of the early squatters had to leave their land, as most could not afford the $2.00 per acre. In 1796 the minimum tract of land that the government would sell was 640 acres, which put the price of land far above what the average pioneer could afford. The Harrison Land Act of 1800 reduced this amount to 320 acres, which was still more than most cash strapped pioneers could pay. Thus, many of those moving into the area before 1801 had to leave their homesteads when others purchased the land.

The Gore

When the Indiana Territory formed in 1800, the region that is now Dearborn County remained part of the Northwest Territory which had Cincinnati as its capitol. It lay west of the Prime Meridian surveyed by Israel Ludlow in 1798. The triangular area of land west of this line included all of what is now Dearborn and Ohio Counties, was called the Gore. Parts of Switzerland, Ripley, Franklin, Wayne, Union and Randolph Counties were also in the Gore. When Congress passed the enabling act on April 2, 1802, that allowed Ohio to begin the statehood process, they detached the Gore from the Northwest Territory and attached it to the Indiana Territory. The Prime Meridian surveyed by Ludlow in 1798 became the line separating Ohio from the Indiana Territory.

Formation of Dearborn County

Indiana Territorial Governor William Henry Harrison attached the region that became Dearborn County to Wayne County on January 24, 1803. Before this the region had no governmental organization. Harrison organized Dearborn County on March 7, 1803, naming it after Dr. Henry Dearborn who served as President Thomas Jefferson's Secretary of War at the time Harrison formed the county. The first court took place in September 1803. One of the earliest offenders was found guilty of striking a judge with a clap board. His sentence included confinement in a pen constructed of logs and rails. His neck was placed in a stock made from two wooden rails. The first Dearborn County jail was built in 1804. The county line followed the Greenville Treaty line, which separated it from Jefferson County. The original Dearborn County included current Ohio and Franklin Counties.

Lawrenceburg County Seat

Harrison deemed Lawrenceburg, platted in 1802, as the county seat. Lawrenceburg would remain the county seat until 1835, when it moved to Wilmington. The county seat remained in Wilmington for eight years.

Separation

Franklin County was separated from Dearborn County in 1811, establishing the current northern boundary. Ripley County separated from Dearborn County 1818Disputes between Rising Sun and Lawrenceburg over the location of the county seat caused the county seat to be moved from Lawrenceburg to Wilmington in 1835, as that town was closer to the center of the county. A new brick court house was constructed in Wilmington. Ohio County was created and separated from Dearborn County in 1844 and the Dearborn County seat shifted back to Lawrenceburg.

Henry Dearborn (Feb. 23, 1751-June 6, 1829)

The son of Simon Dearborn and his wife Sarah Marston, Henry was a native of Hampton, Massachusetts. After attending local schools, Dearborn studied medicine under Dr. Hall Jackson of Portsmouth. After his apprenticeship to Dr. Hall completed he opened a medical practice in 1772.

Revolutionary War

After hostilities broke out in 1776, he recruited a company of militia and served as its captain. He and his company traveled to Bunker Hill and took part in the fight there. His company next participated in the 1775 Quebec campaign with Benedict Arnold, during which the British captured him. They exchanged him in March 1777. Later that year he fought at the Battle of Freeman Farm, the Battle of Saratoga and the Battle of Saratoga. He gained promotion to lieutenant colonel and endured the winter of 177 - 1778 at Valley Forge. Other actions included the 1778 Battle of Monmouth 1779 Sullivan Expedition that fought against the Iroquois in northern New York. In 1781 General George Washington appointed him as deputy quartermaster general on his staff with the rank of colonel. In June 1783 he received his discharge and migrated to Gardiner, Maine to serve as U. S. Marshal for the District of Maine, which was still part of Massachusetts.

Secretary of War

President Thomas Jefferson appointed him Secretary of War at the beginning of his term in 1801. He served the entirety of Jefferson's term in that capacity. During his term he planned the Amerindian removal from the east to areas beyond the Mississippi River.

War of 1812

During the War of 1812 he received appointment as a major general in the United States Army in charge of planning the American assault on Montreal, Kingston, Fort Niagara, and Detroit. His tenure proved ineffective leading to his recall from the frontier and reassignment to an administrative post. He received an honorable discharge from the army on June 15, 1815. President James Madison later submitted Dearborn as a candidate for the Secretary of War position, however the Senate did not confirm the nomination.

Later Life

President James Monroe appointed him as Minister to Portugal, a post he held until 1824, when he requested recall. He died five years later and is interred in Forest Hills Cemetery, which is near Boston.

Dearborn County Court House

April 13, 1871 - Cornerstone Laid for the New Dearborn County Courthouse

Dearborn County officials laid the cornerstone for Dearborn County's fourth court house at a festive ceremony on April 13, 1871. The new courthouse would replace the first one, built in 1810, that had been gutted by a fire.

The First Court House

Built in 1810, the first Dearborn County Court House was a two story brick structure that mimicked the standard court house design of that period. It had a hip roof and octagonal cupola. This courthouse burned on March 26, 1826. Only the brick shell remained.

The "Second" Court House

Most of the county records burned in the fire so county officials asked Dearborn County residents to bring their deeds and other public records to Lawrenceburg to copy them by hand into the records. County commissioners decided not to build a new structure. They decided to use the exterior walls to house the building, constructing a new interior within the burned out walls. This building opened in 1828. The commissions authorized two annex buildings nearby to house the county clerk and the treasurer.

The Third Court House

On September 26, 1836 the county seat moved to Wilmington where it remained until it moved back to Lawrenceburg on January 4, 1844, when Indiana Governor James Whitcomb signed a law authorizing the creation of Ohio County and along with it the relocation of the county seat from Wilmington to Lawrenceburg.

The New Court House

By 1870 Dearborn County needed a new court house. The needs of the county had outgrown the capacity of the old court house. The commissioners inspected several Indiana court houses and decided they liked the Floyd County court house the best. The contacted the architect that designed it, George H. Kyle to design the new one. Mr. Kyle, a Virginia native living in Vevay since about 1840, had designed other court houses and had built up an excellent reputation. He drew up plans which the commissioners accepted on June 15, 1870. Construction of the structure took three years and was completed in 1873. The cost of the courthouse was $135,775.00. During the construction county functions took place in the Odd Fellows building at the intersection of High and Walnut Streets.

Cornerstone Ceremonies

The cornerstone laying ceremony took place with an estimated 5,000 spectators on April 13, 1871 and included guest speaker Louis Jordan. County officials included a time capsule in the cornerstone in which they secreted many items from the period. These included histories of the Masons, Odd Fellows, Druids, Good Templars as well as Lawrenceburg religious societies. They also inserted other historic documents, continental money and old coins from the Revolution.

Completion of the Court House

Workers completed construction in 1873. During the three years construction the Odd Fellows Hall served as the temporary Court House. The building cost $135,775.00 to build. It was a three story building that included city hall offices and a public opera house. The magnificent court room occupied the back half of the second floor. Built from pearl gray limestone quarried at Ellettsville, Indiana the Greek Revival three structure features four fluted columns and an arched doorway. Most of the interior features of the Court House have remained unchanged from the original structure, including the wooden and iron doors and the folding iron window shutters. Five rooms in the court house retain their original fireplaces. The court house included city offices, an opera house and a seventy foot long by fifty foot wide court room on the second floor. Community public ceremonies took place in the court room and included high school graduations and political rallies. The court room was divided in 1903 by order of Judge George E. Downey .

Listed on the National Register of Historic Places on April 9, 1981.

Reference # 81000008

Dearborn County Courthouse

Corner of High and Mary Streets

Lawrenceburg, IN

http://www.dearborncounty.org

Townships

Caesar Creek - Established - 1826

Center - Established - 1839

Clay - Established - 1835

Harrison - Established - 1844

Hogan - Established - 1844

Jackson - Established - 1832

Kelso - Established - 1826

Lawrenceburg - Established - 1803

Logan - Established - 1836

Manchester - Established - c. 1803

Miller - Established - 1834

Sparta - Established - c. 1826

Washington - Established - 1852

York - Established – 1841

Incorporated Cities and Towns

Aurora

Area - Total - 3.09 sq mi

Elevation - 486 ft

Population - 3,687 (2018)

ZIP code – 47001

Administration Building

235 Main Street

812-926-1777

https://www.aurora.in.us/

Aurora is a southeastern Indiana town on the Ohio River. Located on US 50, Indiana State Roads 148, 56 and 350 begin their westward journey in Aurora. Indiana State Road 350 connects Aurora with Osgood, Indiana to the west. Indiana State Road 56 links it to Rising Sun, Indiana to the west. Indiana State Road 148 connects with Indiana State Road 48 a few miles north of Aurora.

Thumbnail History

Historical lore places Adam Flake as the first resident of the future site of Aurora who built a cabin in January 1796.

The town saw some settlement as early as 1796. An engagement of the Revolutionary War took place on the banks of nearby Laughery Creek. On August 24, 1781 Chief Joseph Brant, a leader of the Mohawk Indians, intercepted Colonel Archibald Andrew Lochry near the site of what is now Aurora and massacred or captured the unit under Lochey's command. A memorial is located at River view Cemetery in Aurora.

For more information on this incident, see the entry in the Historical Marker section.

Platted in 1819, Aurora derives its name from Aurora, the Roman goddess of dawn. Trustee Jesse L. Holman filed the plat on January 14, 1819. Cincinnati resident Charles Vattier purchased the land from the United States Government on September 18, 1804. Dearborn county residents purchased the land from Vattier in 1819. The plat marked 206 lots and six public squares. The first public auction of lots in Aurora took place on April 13, 1819. Aurora, Indiana has a history as an important river port on the Ohio River. River View Cemetery

Established in 1869 on the banks of Laughery Creek on the site of Lochrey's Massacre, the thirty-acre cemetery includes a historical marking the massacre and contains the graves of over 13,000 people. Located at the intersection of Indiana State Road 56 and East Laughery Road, the cemetery is a serene resting place.

Aurora Ferry

Shortly after the town's founding, Aurora granted a license to operate a ferry to Boone County, Kentucky to one Phillip Craig in 1819. Early ferries provided a much-needed link between Aurora and Kentucky, across the Ohio River. Horses walking on a treadmill provided power for a pair of side mounted paddle to the early ferries. The Aurora ferry would have horses providing power for the ferry until an ice gorge destroyed the ferry in 1918. The ferry operated until 1978 when the I-275 Bridge made it unprofitable.

Aurora Railroad Depot

The railroad depot was established on land originally settled by Scot John Gillis in the 1890's. Gills, a veteran of the American Revolution, constructed a two-room cabin on the site that the depot currently occupies. The Ohio & Mississippi

Railroad Depot purchased the property in 1853. The first train departed for Cochran Indiana on April 4, 1854.

Jesse Lynch Holman (October 24, 1784 – March 18, 1842)

The son of Henry Holeman and Jane Gordon, Jessy was a native of the frontier near Danville, Kentucky. After reading law, the Kentucky bar admitted him in 1805. Holman practiced law first at Carrollton, Kentucky. After moving to New Castle and Frankfort, he moved to a site near current Aurora, Indiana in 1811. He built a two story log home overlooking the Ohio River he called Veraestau.

Politics and Law

Indiana Territorial Governor William Henry Harrison appointed Holman as prosecuting attorney for Dearborn County and judge of the second judicial circuit in 1814. He also served as a member of the Territorial legislative assembly. After statehood, he served on the circuit court and on the Indiana Supreme court until 1830.

Return to Private Life

He went back to Verastau in 1831 to reopen his law office. Holman became an ordained Baptist minister in 1834, after an unsuccessful bid for the United States Senate. His later efforts led to the founding of Indiana University, Franklin College, and the Indiana Historical Society. He also wrote a novel, The Prisoners of the Niagara. This was published in 1810. He founded the Indiana Bible Society on June 4, 1831.

Federal Judge

Holman's last public post was as appointee to the U.S. District Court for the District of Indiana by President Andrew Jackson in 1835. He held this post until his death in 1842.

For more historical information on Aurora, see the Downtown Aurora National Historical Area later in this book.

Greendale, Indiana

County - Dearborn

Area Total - 6.1 sq. mi

Elevation - 528 ft

Population - 4,373 (2018)

ZIP code - 47025

Area code(s) - 812

Thumbnail History

Revolutionary war veteran Captain John Crandall settled on the ridge above the Ohio River, and then called Pleasant Ridge, shortly after the 1795 Treaty of Greenville between General Anthony Wayne and the various Amerindian tribes of current Indiana and Ohio. George Rabb, another early settler, also established himself on the Ridge. Stephen Ludlow platted Greendale, Indiana in 1852 on a high ridge that overlooks the Ohio River Valley. It is adjacent to Lawrenceburg, Indiana that it also overlooks. Greendale has four public parks. Dearborn Trail begins at the intersection of East William and High Street in Greendale.

State Road 1 creases the north edge of the town as it wends its way to State Road 46 and Interstate 74. Indiana State Road 1 begins at an intersection with US Route 50 on the south edge of town. An interchange at the intersection of Indiana State Road 1 also connects the highway to I-275, which provides access to I-75 and I-71.

For dining, lodging and shopping opportunities in Greendale, contact:

City of Greendale

500 Ridge Avenue

Greendale, IN 47025

812-537-9219

info@cityofgreendale.net

http://www.cityofgreendale.net

Lawrenceburg, Indiana

County - Dearborn

Area Total - 5.0 sq. mi (13.1 km2)

Elevation - 479 ft (146 m)

Population (2016) Total 4,968

ZIP code 47025

Area code(s) 812

Surveyors William Vance, James Hamilton and Benjamin Chambers laid out the town of Lawrenceburg in April 1802. Vance had settled in the Cincinnati and became familiar with the best sites along the Ohio River. He decided that a site just west of the junction of the Miami River and the Ohio River would be an ideal site for a city.

Dearborn County

Samuel Vance (1770-1830)

The son of William Vance and Sarah Colville Vance, Samuel was native to Bath, Pennsylvania. He trained as a surveyor and migrated to Cincinnati, Ohio sometime before 1803. During that year married Mary Morris Lawrence, the granddaughter of General and Northwest Territory governor Arthur St. Clair. The couple had nine children. Vance served under General Anthony Wayne in the

Northwest Indian Wars and served on the board of the Indiana Canal Company at its formation in 1805. Vance also fought in the War of 1812. he settled permanently in Lawrenceburg in 1818. Vance purchased the land that would become Lawrenceburg at the Cincinnati Land Office. Vance surveyed the town of Lawrenceburg in April 1802, using his wife's maiden name to name the town.

Important Transportation Hub

The city was an important city early in the state's history due to its location on the Ohio River. It became an important railroad center as well, and two rail lines, the Central Railroad Co. of Indiana and the CSX Transportation Inc. still run through the city. Lawrenceburg also served as the southern terminus of the Whitewater Canal, built in the 1840's. The downtown area borders the shoreline of the Ohio River that you may see from the Levee Walk that is located at the end of Walnut Street. The Levee Walk is a part of the longer trail that leads to Aurora to the west. Lawrenceburg, Indiana has one major highway, US 50, connecting it with Aurora, Versailles, Seymour and Vincennes to the west and Cincinnati, Ohio to the east. Indiana State Road 48 connects to US 50, providing access to central Ripley County to the northwest.

For more information about shopping, dining and lodging in Lawrenceburg, contact the Dearborn County Visitor Center.

For more historical information on Lawrenceburg, see the Downtown Lawrenceburg National Historical Area later in this book.

Dearborn County Visitor Center

320 Walnut Street

Lawrenceburg, IN 47025

Phone: 812-537-0814

Toll Free: 800-322-8198

E-mail: dearborn@visitsoutheastindiana.com

https://www.visitsoutheastindiana.com

Dillsboro, Indiana

County - Dearborn

Township - Clay

Area - 1.0 sq. mile

Elevation 869 ft.

Population - 1,401 (2018)

ZIP code 47018

Area code(s) 812

Thumbnail History

Early settlers to southeast Indiana settled along the Laughery Creek valley. Sometime in 1816, a group of settlers from Springfield, Ohio filtered into the area that became Dillsboro. Mathias Whetstone laid out Dillsboro on March 16, 1830. The plat included sixteen lots. William Williamson donated land for a log church, which became the Hopewell Presbyterian Church sometime around 1826. The cemetery remains, however the congregation moved to Dillsboro later on.

The building of a post road in the late 1820's created an ideal spot for a town to grow about an hour west of Cincinnati. town was named after a local man, General James Dill who served in the War of 1812.

The post road was incorporated into the United States Federal Highway System in 1923 and became US 50, which passes just north of the town now, due to a bypass which was constructed in the 1950's. Indiana State Roads 62 and 262 pass through the town.

James Dill (c. 1778 - August 18, 1838)

The son of Thomas Dill and Rebecca Dill, James was native to Belfast, Ireland. Dill migrated to the United States shortly after the Revolutionary War ended. After his arrival, he settled in the Northwest Territory and became friends with Indiana Territorial Governor William Henry Harrison and married former Northwest Territory Governor, General Arthur St. Clair's daughter Elizabeth St Clair . An attorney, Dill was one of the earliest members of the Dearborn County bar. Dill served during the War of 1812 as a general and after the war served as speaker of the Indiana Territorial Assembly.

General Dill was a part of the Indiana Constitutional Convention in 1816 in Corydon, Indiana, serving as Dearborn County's representative. Dill was Clerk of the Circuit Court at the time of Dillsboro's founding and was also the first Dearborn County Recorder.

Moore's Hill, Indiana

County - Dearborn

Township - Sparta

Area Total - 0.5 sq. mi

Elevation 991 ft

Population (2000)

Total 635

ZIP code 47032

Area code(s) 812

Alan Moore, owner of Moore's Mill, and Andrew Stevens platted the town of Moore's Hill in 1839. It consisted of the gristmill and nine lots. Moore's Hill College opened its doors as a denominational college in 1907. In 1908, Carnegie Hall was constructed by the university to serve as an academic building. It later served as an elementary and high school. It is now utilized as a museum. The college survived until 1917 when it relocated to Evansville and became Evansville University.

For more about Carnegie Hall, see the National Historic Register article.

Saint Leon, Indiana

County - Dearborn

Area – Total - 6.99 sq. mi

Population (2010) - 678

Area code - 812

Located at the intersection of Indiana State Roads 46 and 1, St. Leon also has access to Interstate 74 at Exit 164. Local lore suggests that the town derives its name from r St. Leon Bembo. The town's Pole Raising event has become famous state wide as the only remaining pole raising ceremony in Indiana.

St. Leon Bembo (Birth Date Unknown - c. 1188)

Leon Bembo was a Catholic Saint born in Venice, Italy. He served as a diplomat to one of the Doge's of Venice. The Doge was the title of an elected leader who served for life. St. Leon was injured in religious riots, after which he retired to a monastery.

Pole Raising

St. Leon is the only town in Indiana that still holds a "Pole Raising," ceremony. The Pole Raising is a quadrennial event that takes place during Presidential election years. Drawn from the traditional "Liberty Pole," of the years predating the American Revolution, the Pole Raising became popular in the Presidential election of Democrat Andrew Jackson and National Republican (Whig) John Q. Adams. The Democrats used a hickory pole, in honor of their candidate's nickname, Old Hickory. The Democrats first used the donkey as a symbol during this election. The symbol originated when the opposition Whigs labeled Jackson a jackass. The Democrats adopted the symbol unofficially during that election. It became the official symbol in 1870. The Whigs adopted a yellow poplar (Liriodendron tulipfera) as their pole and the log cabin as their symbol. The Pole Raising became a popular quadrennial event during the remainder of the Nineteenth and early Twentieth Centuries. Parades, barbeques and other political speeches accompanied the pole-raising event. The St. Leon Pole Raising uses a former Democratic emblem with Indiana roots, the Rooster.

Liberty Pole

Typically, a Liberty Pole was a tall wooden pole with a Phrygian Cap on top. A Phrygian Cap was a cap worn by freed slaves in Rome. The symbol arose in 44 BC after the assassination of Emperor Julius Caesar. A Liberty Pole marked a meeting place of the Sons of Liberty and was a symbol of their protests. British troops frequently cut these poles down, which was a highly provocative act.

St. Leon Pole Raising

Since this is a Democratic Party event, a traditional hickory pole is used. During the morning of the event residents trek into the woods, choose a hickory tree, and cut it down using the traditional crosscut saw. They fasten a flag with the

Rooster emblem to the pole, as well as an American Flag. They suspend the pole between two wagons, after carrying it back into town, and parade it through the streets. After the parade, workers raise the pole using traditional rope methods to a chorus of cheers. The pole remains in place until Election Day. For more information on the St. Leon Pole Raising, contact:

St. Leon Pole Raising

http://dearborncountydemocrats.com/poll-raising/

The Democratic Rooster

The Indiana Whig's derisive chant to their opponent, Joseph Chapman during the 1840 elections turned into an emblem for the Indiana Democratic Party and later the National Party.

Joseph Chapman

A native of Ohio, Chapman migrated to Indiana to Rush County. In 1829 he moved to Hancock County where built the first tavern in the new town of Greenfield in 1834. He married twice, the first time to Jane Curry, with whom he had six children. Mrs. Curry passed away and he married Matilda Agnes. That union produced five children. He entered politics as a Jacksonian Democrat and won the 1832 election as town clerk. In 1837, he gained election to the Indiana House of Representatives. He won reelection four times. His 1840 election produced the Democratic Party emblem.

"Crow, Chapman, Crow!"

Chapman gained renown for his boasting style of speech. The term for boasting at the time was to accuse someone of "crowing," in reference to the raucous bird. When Chapman would speak, the Whigs took up the derisive chant, "Crow, Chapman, Crow." The Democrats picked up on this and turned it around, using the crow as the emblem for his campaign. Chapman won that election, prompting the Indiana Democrats to adopt the symbol. The National Democrats soon adopted it. Though the jackass, first used on Democrats during Andrew Jackson's campaign in 1828, became the unofficial emblem in 1870, the rooster still saw use after that. As late as 1944, Franklin Roosevelt still used it. Many Democrats still use the emblem in some areas of the United States.

Dearborn County has erected an historical marker honoring the event.

Text:

On this site, since 1892, during each Presidential election campaign, a tall hickory pole bearing an American Flag and Democrat "Rooster," is raised by manpower alone. Once widespread custom dating from 1828 campaign of Andrew "Old Hickory," Jackson.

Saint Leon

7282 Church Lane

West Harrison, IN 47060

(812) 576-5368

http://www.stleon.us/index.htm

West Harrison

West Harrison, Indiana

Area - Total - 0.23 sq mi

Elevation - 518 ft

Population (2010) - 289

ZIP code - 47060

Area code - 812

Laid out in mid to late December 1813, West Harrison is the sister city to Harrison, Ohio, located across the Indiana/Ohio State line. It is about eighteen miles from Lawrenceburg, Indiana, via I-274 and I-74. Early settlers in the area found numerous Indian mounds scattered across the landscape. Most of the early building lots had the remains of these mounds.

West Harrison, Indiana sits on the banks of the Whitewater River on the Indiana/Ohio State Line just west of Harrison, Ohio. State Street, which runs on a north south axis, is the state line and the official boundary between the two towns.

The Indiana and Ohio Railroad runs through West Harrison as it connects Cincinnati, Ohio with Brookville, Indiana.

West Harrison has access to Interstate 74 and US 52 via State Street/Old Highway 52, which joins the Interstate, and the US Highway.

Town of West Harrison

Town Hall

100 Railroad Ave.

West Harrison, Indiana

(812) 637-5261

http://www.townofwestharrison.org

Census-Designated Places

Bright

Hidden Valley

Bright, Indiana

County - Dearborn

Area

Total - 14.3 sq mi

Elevation - 922 ft

Population (2010)

Total - 5,693

Area code(s) 812

Latitude 39.2184 and longitude -84.8561

The United States Postal Service established a post office in Bright in 1847, however in 1904 the office was closed.

Bright, Indiana is one of the more isolated communities in Indiana. No major highways go there, access is only by county roads. There are no railroads or interstates nearby. However, it is in a beautiful area of the state, and in the Cincinnati metropolitan area. It is a growing town with many advantages despite is remote location. You get there by traveling State Line Road about six miles from its intersection with US 50 about 2.3 miles east of its intersection with Indiana State Road 1. Another way is to take North Dearborn Road east from its intersection with Indiana State Road 1 in Dover. State Line Road intersects North Dearborn Road about 5.94 miles east of this intersection. Bright is about 1.4 miles south of North Dearborn Road.

Bright Indiana

http://www.brightin.org/wordpress/

Hidden Valley

Townships

Miller, Lawrenceburg

Area - Total - 4.4 sq mi (11.4 km2)

Land - 4.1 sq mi (10.7 km2)

Water - 0.3 sq mi (0.7 km2)

Elevation - 548 ft (167 m)

Population - (2010) - 5,387

Doublelick Run serves as the stream that feeds Hidden Valley Lake. Located between State Line Road, Georgetown Road and Indiana State Road 101, Hidden Valley is near the Ohio State Line and south of Bright. Ohio land developer Jacob Rupel began developing Hidden Valley Lake in 1970. To build the lake, which is the deepest lake in Indiana, he built Indiana's second largest dam. He first offered 300 lots. An additional 2000+ lots became available in 1972.

Hidden Valley Lake

150 acres

1.5 miles long

4.5 miles of shoreline

120 feet max depth

45 feet average depth

2,059,378,320 gal. storage when full

Hidden Valley Dam

Height – 140 feet

Length – 1195 foot

Top width – 28 feet

Base width – 732 feet

Compacted fill – 1,212, 890 cu. yds.

Hidden Valley Lake

Property Owners Association

19303 Schmarr Drive

Lawrenceburg, IN 47025

Phone: 812-537-3091

hiddenvalleylakeindiana@comcast.net

https://hiddenvalleylakeindiana.com/community/

Unincorporated Communities

Bonnell

Braysville

Chesterville

Cochran

Cold Springs

Dover

Farmers Retreat

Guilford

Hardinsburg

Hubbells Corner

Kyle

Lawrenceburg Junction

Lawrenceville

Logan

Manchester

Mount Sinai

New Alsace

Petersburg

Sparta

Weisburg

Wilmington

Wrights Corner

Utah

Wilmington

Yorkville

Wrights Corner

Bonnell

Located at the intersection of Bonnell Road and Konradi Road northeast of Indiana State Road 48, Bonnell was a railroad town in the mid 1880's. The West Fork of Tanner's Creek flows south of the now defunct town. Ziegler Creek joins with Tanner's Creek at the town's site. Established as Kennedy, the post office opened on November 5, 1885. The Post Office remained open until 1929. The town's original name derived from a railroad official that worked for the rail line that ran through the town. Another railroad official provided the new name, Bonnell, later on. Driven by the activity of the railroad, the town grew to eventually include the Clissman sawmill, a church, several stores, a stockyard and a train depot. The nearby Turkey Point Schoolhouse provided an education for Bonnell children. The schoolhouse still exists on Turkey Point Road, which is a dead end road now. A pumphouse located on Burtzelebach pumped water from the West Fork of Tanner's Creek to supply the steam powered locomotives that traveled through Bonnell. Mount Hope Church established in 1896. The steel truss bridge built in 1914 over West Fork of Tanner's Creek. The current bridge replaced it in the 1990's. The advent of the automobile caused the eventual decline of the passenger train, which in turn led to the decline of Bonnell, as it did many other small railroad towns. To get to Bonnell, drive north from Manchester on North Manchester Road to Amm Road and turn right. At the intersection of Amm Road and Platt Road, turn left. Turn right at the intersection with Konradi Road. The ghost town of Bonnell is at the Konradi Road and Bonnell Road.

Braysville

Located on US Route 52 about a half mile from its intersection with Indiana State Road 46, Braysville had a post office from 1853 until 1861.

Chesterville

Township - Sparta

Elevation - 873 ft

ZIP code - 47032

Located about 4 miles southeast of Moore's Hill at the intersection of Chesterville Road and Longbranch Road, Chesterville had a post office from 1884 until 1907.

Cochran

Named for founder George W. Cochran, was laid out in in 1860. The plat was filed with the recorder's office on August 25, 1860. The B & O Southwestern Railway built shops in the fledgling town to repair locomotives. The Aurora and Laughery Turnpike formed the main street of the town. When the railroad moved its repair shops to Washington, Indiana the town withered away. The first postmaster was A. P. Shutts. Cochran had a post office from 1878 - 1917. Roughly bounded by Conwell Street, Railroad Avenue and Indiana Avenue, Cochran is located within the city limits of Aurora.

Cold Springs

Township - Sparta

Elevation - 787 ft

ZIP code - 47032

Latitude/Longitude - 39°04'17?N - 85°04'23?W.

Located about 1 mile west of Chesterville Road on Cold Springs Road, the town was a shipping point for farmer's goods for the Baltimore and Ohio Railroad. Cold Springs is in southwestern Dearborn county.

Dover, Indiana

Elevation - 938 ft

ZIP code - 47022

First settled in 1815, Dover is located at the intersection of Indiana State Road 1 and North Dearborn Road. Confederate General John T. Morgan and his troops passed through Dover on July 13, 1863 as he passed through southern Indiana on his way to Ohio. Dover is also home to the second oldest Roman Catholic church in Indiana, St. John The Baptist Church. Dearborn County has placed two historical markers in Dover that tell the story of Morgan and the Church. For more information on the church, see the Dearborn County historical marker section.

Farmers Retreat

County - Dearborn

Township - Caesar Creek

Elevation - 879 ft

ZIP code - 47018

Located at the intersection of Indiana State Road 62 and Bell's Branch Road, Farmer's Retreat occupies a site in north central Caesar Creek Township. A post office operated from the town's founding in 1852 until 1925. Originally called Opptown, the new name of Farmer's Retreat originated when General John Hunt Morgan staged his raid across southern Indiana. Farmers in the region, upon hearing rumors of Morgan's advance, retreated into the woods to hide their horses from Morgan's men.

Guilford, Indiana

County - Dearborn

Township - York

Elevation - 499 ft

ZIP code - 47022

Population - (York Township) - 1,221

Guilford History

Guilford is an unincorporated town in York Township, Dearborn County, Indiana. It is located at the forks of Tanners Creek. Charles L. and Josiah Campbell discovered that a railroad was soon to be built in the area and platted Guilford in 1850. The railroad created a town that was attractive to settlement and commerce. In 1875, Guilford boasted an Odd Fellows Hall, a Grange Hall, a school and a small railroad station.

Telephone Exchange and Post Office

Guilford is the only unincorporated community in Dearborn County that has its own telephone exchange prefix, (487), and its own post office, which was established at the forks of Tanners Creek in 1841.

Hardinsburg

Township - Lawrenceburg

Elevation - 486 ft (148 m)

ZIP code - 47025

Platted in 1815 Hardinsburg derives its name from the original owner of the land, Henry Hardin. The village had a post office from 1820 through 1836. Located southeast of the intersection of US Route 50 and Indiana State Road 101, Hardinsburg is at the northern terminus of the Greendale Trail.

Hubbell's Corner

Located at the intersection of Lawrenceville Road and North Dearborn Road, the town derives its name from merchant Merritt Hubbell.

Kyle

Township - Manchester

Elevation - 906 ft (276 m)

ZIP code - 47001

Located at the intersection of Indiana State Road 48 and Ellinghausen Road, Kyle had a post office from 1883 until 1904.

Lawrenceburg Junction

Located on Oberting Road about 1.07 miles from its intersection with US Route 50 along the Central Railroad line, Lawrenceburg Junction derives its name from nearby Lawrenceburg.

Lawrenceville

Township - Jackson

Elevation - 961 ft (293 m)

ZIP code - 47041

Located at the intersection of Indiana State Road 46 and Lawrenceville Road, Lawrenceville had a post office from 1846 through 1904. Jonathan Lawrence platted the town in 1830.

Logan

Township - Logan

Elevation - 922 ft (281 m)

ZIP code - 47022

Deriving its name from Logan Township, Logan had a post office from 1836 until 1927. It is located at the intersection of Mount Pleasant Road and North Dearborn Road.

Manchester

Township - Manchester

Elevation - 919 ft (280 m)

ZIP code - 47041

Deriving its name from Manchester Township, a post office existed here from 1822 until 1914. Manchester is located at the intersection of Indiana State Road 48 and County Farm Road.

Mount Sinai

Township - Hogan

Elevation - 873 ft (266 m)

ZIP code - 47032

Mount Sinai derives its name from Mount Sinai Methodist Episcopal Church, which was built in 1835. The village is located at the intersection of Mt. Sinai Road and Indiana State Road 350.

New Alsace

Township - Kelso

Elevation - 955 ft (291 m)

ZIP code - 47041

Deriving its name from the native region of some of the early settlers, Alsace, New Alsace was platted in 1838. A post office was in the town from 1845 until 1904. It is at the junction of Legion, Graf and North Dearborn Roads.

Sparta

Township - Sparta

Elevation - 915 ft (279 m)

ZIP code - 47032

Located at the intersection of Rummel Road and Indiana State Road 350, Sparta had a post office from 1846 until 1904.

Utah

Located near the intersection of George Street and Eads Avenue in Lawrenceburg, the site's name likely derives from the Utah Territory.

Weisburg

Township - Jackson

Elevation - 932 ft (284 m)

ZIP code - 47041

Gristmill owner Philip Weis laid the town out in 1858. It is located on the West Fork of Tanners Creek where Weisburg Road crosses it just south of Hubble's Corner.

Wrights Corner

Township - Manchester

Elevation - 906 ft (276 m)

ZIP code - 47022

Wrights Corner derives its name from local general store owner and postmaster Washington Wright. The post office was established in 1853 and closed in 1903. The town is located at the intersection of Kaiser Drive and Indiana State Road 48.

Dearborn County National Register of Historic Places

George Street Bridge

Listed on the National Register of Historic Places

March 1, 1984

Reference # 84001012

Dearborn County Bridge #159

constructed in 1887 by the Lomas Forge and Bridge Works of Cincinnati, Ohio the George Street bridge carried traffic on George Street over Tanner Creek. An important gateway into downtown Aurora, the George Street Bridge has been closed to vehicular traffic, however it still serves as a pedestrian walkway across the creek. The design utilized a design, the Whipple truss, patented by Squire Whipple in 1847. Three bridges of this type still exist in Dearborn County.

Squire Whipple (September 16, 1804 – March 15, 1888)

The son of the son of James and Electa Johnson Whipple, Native to Hardwick, Massachusetts. Whipple's family migrated to New York about 1817. He attended Fairfield Academy in Herkimer, New York and later Union College. His father designed, constructed and operated a cotton-spinning mill in Greenwich, Massachusetts. His father's project exposed the growing boy to construction and design. After graduating in one year, Whipple served as an apprentice for various railroads, designing and selling precision instruments like surveying transits and drafting equipment in his spare time. He became an early advocate for using iron to build bridges. Many at the time did not trust iron for use in bridges. He patented his first iron bridge design in 1841, a design known as the bowstring iron truss. He used this design to build his first bridge in 1841. He had constructed a prototype of his design at his own expense, which convinced the commissioners of the of the Erie Canal to try his design. In 1847 Whipple designed a variation of the Pratt truss bridge design, which has become known as the Whipple truss bridge. His design, along with his book, A Work on Bridge Building, appeared that same year. His influence in bridge design and construction led to his unofficial moniker, "the father of iron bridge," construction in the United States. He was the first engineer to develop scientifically based rules for bridge construction.

After his death in 1888 he was interred in Albany Rural Cemetery, Menands, New York.

Hamline Chapel United Methodist Church

Listed on the National Register of Historic Places

September 9, 1982

Reference # 82000030

Constructed in 1847 on High Street the Greek Revival architecture church has served the needs of its congregation since that time. Its prominent location on an elevated site has protected it from many of the Ohio River floods over the years. A levee constructed after the 1937 flood protects the church now. Located just a short distance from the location of Lawrenceburg's early Ohio River wharves, the church's elevated position made it a navigational aid to boats traveling the river. The Methodist congregation had the church constructed after it outgrew its original Walnut Street church.

Laughery Creek Road Bridge

Abandoned in 1993, this bridge carried East Laughery Creek Road across a small tributary of Laughery Creek. The bridge is 41 feet long, 16 feet wide with its longest span of 39 feet.

Constructed in 1917, it is a metal 3 Panel Rivet-Connected fixed Warren Pony Truss bridge. It is located a short distance northwest of Riverview Cemetery.

Listed on the National Register of Historic Places on September 29, 1976.

Reference # 76000018

Daniel S. Major House

Listed on the National Register of Historic Place

December 23, 2003

Reference # 03001320

Located at 761 West Eads Parkway, Lawrenceburg, Indiana,

Constructed between 1857 - 1860 for real estate developer Daniel Symmes Major , the two story Italianate style house sits on just over 18 acres overlooking the main road that traveled between Aurora and Lawrenceburg.

Daniel Symmes Major (September 6, 1808 - September 23, 1872)

Daniel Symmes Major moved to Lawrenceburg, Indiana in 1831 after graduating from V in Oxford, Ohio. He studied law with General James Dill, gaining admittance to the bar in 1832. The next year Symmes married Catherine Eliza Guard Major with whom he had five children. Sometime in the 1840's he began speculating in real estate and by 1860 had sold over 120 Lawrenceburg city lots and conducted the drawing of two subdivision plats.

His family had lived on High Street in Lawrenceburg, however they sold that property in 1859 and moved into the home the next year.

After his death in 1872 he was interred in Greendale Cemetery in Greendale, Indiana.

Lewis Hurlbert Sr. House

Listed National Register of Historic Places

November 25, 1994

Reference # 94001350

Lewis Hurlbert constructed the two story Greek Revival architectural style with Italianate detailing in 1844. the north side of the home faces the Ohio River, which due to its elevated location, provided a commanding view of the river.

Lewis Gordon Hurlbert Sr. (August 14, 1814 - December 29, 1873)

The son of Truman and Polly Rush Hurlbert, Lewis was native to Albany, New York. While a young man, Lewis traveled to Boston, Massachusetts and then to New Orleans. In 1835 he migrated to Aurora.

Lewis and Emma Leah Conwell married in Napoleon, Indiana in February 16, 1837. The couple would have six children. Miss Conwell was the daughter of one of Aurora's founders Elias Conwell, who owned property in Aurora, but had moved to Napoleon, Indiana in 1821. Hurlbert had the home at 408-498 Bridgeway Street constructed in 1844.

In 1848 Hurlbert established the first lumber business in Aurora, dealing in rough and dressed lumber purchased from suppliers in Michigan. In addition to lumber the company sold shingles, sashes, doors and other building materials. The company prospered and grew, occupying several city blocks an operating a planing mill. At his death in 1873 Lewis Sr.'s son, Lewis Jr., took over the business.

After his death in 1873 he was interred at River View Cemetery, near Aurora.

Lewis Hurlbert Sr. House

408-498 Bridgeway St,

Aurora, IN 47001

Aurora City Hall

Listed March 14, 1996

Reference # 96000288

The district included in the listing includes two separate buildings at the corner of Third and Main Streets that have been connected. The main two story Romanesque Revival mode building houses city offices and the city council chamber. Constructed in 1887, the City Hall Building has a gabled front and is three bays wide. The architectural firm of McDonald Brothers, Louisville designed the building, which is possibly the third oldest city building in use in Indiana. Prior to the construction of this building, city offices were scattered across the city. The building that houses the Aurora Fire Department was constructed in 1870. The City of Aurora purchased the building for the fire department in 1882. An addition in 1970 joined the two buildings.

Aurora City Hall

237 Main Street

Aurora IN, 47001

Aurora Public Library District

The surveyors that platted Aurora in 1819 reserved space in the plat for a library, calling the street it was to locate Literary street, now Fifth street.

First Libraries

The first library appeared sometime after the founding of the town was probably a subscription library. This library moved to several different locations. The first publicly supported library appeared in 1901, housed in the Aurora City Hall. Miss Georgiana E. Sutton passed away on January 18, 1901. In her will she instructed her brother and executor, Dr. D. H. Sutton to construct a permanent library using funds from her estate. The cost of the new building was not to exceed $10,000. The building was the first structure constructed in Aurora as a dedicated library facility.

Architects Frederick W. Garber and Clifford B. Woodward designed the building after reaching an agreement with the heir of the donor, Miss Georgiana E. Sutton and the Aurora Public Library District in 1913. Construction on the Italian Renaissance Revival design structure commenced in 1913. It was fifty-four feet long, forty-eight feet wide and was "T" shaped. It included a raised basement and limestone foundation. The library held its official opening on October 13, 1914. Nine years later the Library built an addition to the building.

The National Register of Historic Places listed the library on May 27, 1993.

Georgiana E. Sutton (1842 - January 18, 1901)

The daughter of George Sutton and Sarah Sutton, Georgiana was native to Aurora in Dearborn County. A member of a prominent family, Georgiana was a lover of books and education. A world traveler, she became involved in many of the cultural and literary activities in Aurora. The Sutton family immigrated in 1819 and included a number of doctors. The family promoted education in the community and helped establish the public school system in Aurora.

She is interred in River View Cemetery in Aurora.

Frederick W. Garber (July 21, 1877–August 2, 1950)

The son of Friedrich Heinrich Christian and Mary Elise Rabbe Garber, Frederick was native to Cincinnati, Ohio. He studied architecture at Cincinnati Technical School, worked later as a draftsman and continued his architectural education at M. I. T. After finishing at M. I. T. he traveled abroad on a Rotch Scholarship to study in Europe. He and his brother in law, Clifford B. Woodward, established the firm Garber & Woodward architectural firm in 1904. He married Alice Noble Woodward with whom he had one son.

He was a pioneer in the International Style of Architecture in Cincinnati and vicinity.

Frederick is interred at Spring Grove Cemetery in Cincinnati, Ohio.

Garber's projects include:

Woodie Garber residence Glendale, Ohio (1952)

Procter Hall, University of Cincinnati

All Saints Chapel addition, Christ Church Glendale (1959–1960)

Clifford Brooks Woodward (May 13, 1878 - October23, 1954)

The son of Henry Lynde Woodward and Martha Reynolds Thomas, Clifford was native to Cincinnati, Ohio. He studied architecture at the Cincinnati Technical School and at M. I. T. He worked for (Elzner &Anderson from 1897-1901 and with Fred Mueller, Hamilton, Ohio from 1903-1904. In 1904 he joined with his brother in law in their firm, Garber & Woodward.

Structures designed by the firm include:

Union Central Life Insurance Co. Building

Withrow High School Bridge

Anna Louise Inn for Girls

Phoenix Building

In 1988 Caesar Creek, enter, Clay, Hogan, Manchester, Sparta and Washington Township joined the Aurora Public Library district.

The District added a branch in West Harrison, Indiana in 2000. Mr. and Mrs. Robert Dunevant donated the three-acre tract for the library.

Aurora Public Library District

414 Second Street

Aurora, IN 47001

Aurora Public Library District

https://eapld.org/

Hillforest Historic Mansion

Listed on the National Register of Historic Places

August 5, 1971

Reference # 71000005

Hillforest sits on a bluff overlooking the Ohio River. Designed by architect Isaiah Rogers and constructed by industrialist and financier Thomas Gaff in 1855, Hillforest Mansion sits astride a hill that affords a majestic view of the Ohio River.

Thomas Gaff (July 8, 1808 - April 25, 1884)

The son of James and Margaret Wilson Gaff, Thomas was native to Edinburgh, Scotland. His father, a paper maker, moved the family to Springfield, New Jersey. Gaff received his education in private schools and learned papermaking from his father. An uncle, Charles Wilson, taught him the distilling business. Thomas and his brother James founded a distillery in Philadelphia. In 1843, the brothers moved their operation to Aurora, Indiana. Their distillery, called the T & J.W. Gaff & Company Distillery, produced bourbon, rye, and Thistle Dew Scotch whiskey. The business thrived and their business empire expanded to include the Crescent Brewing Company, a Nevada silver mine, farming operations and many others. The Gaffs also owned a fleet of steamboats that they used to transport their various products on the rivers.

Isaiah Rogers (August 17, 1800 – April 13, 1869)

The son of Isaac and Hannah Ford Rogers, Isaiah was native to Marshfield, Massachusetts. A student of famed Massachusetts architect Solomon Willard, Isaiah became a leading architect in the United States. He designed structures in Mobile, Alabama, Boston, New York City, Louisville, Kentucky, and Cincinnati, Ohio. His designs included Boston's Tremont House, New York's Astor House and the Burnett House in Cincinnati.

Hillforest Historic Mansion

Situated on ten acres of land overlooking the Ohio River, Gaff lived in the home until his death in 1884. The Gaff family retained ownership of the home until furniture manufacturer Will Stark purchased the home in 1924. The local chapter of the Veterans of Foreign Wars owned the home, using it as a meeting place, until a group of local citizens purchased the home in 1955. Organizing as the Hillforest Historical Foundation, the group restored the home and opened it for public tours in 1956. The National Historic Landmark Program listed it as a National Historic Landmark in 1992. The restored home is open for tours from April 1 until December 30. The home was designated a National Historic Landmark in 1992.

Hillforest Historic Mansion

213 Fifth St

Aurora, Indiana

812-926-0087

http://www.hillforest.org

Charles Hisey Residence

Charles Hisey had this home constructed in 1918, replacing an earlier home on the site. Iron-filled bricks give the structure its purple coloration.

First Evangelical United Church of Christ

Listed on the National Register of Historic Places

September 23, 1994

Reference # 94001104

Constructed by the Baptists

The Baptists organized in Aurora in 1820, using a log house on Fifth Street as their first meeting place. The congregation, known as the Aurora Baptist

Church, constructed a church, the first permanent one in Aurora, sometime between 1825 and 1828. Jesse L. Holman was the leading figure in the organization of this church. The congregation, then known as the First Baptist Church of Aurora, constructed the Gothic Revival style church on Fifth Street in 1848. Citizens in Aurora purchased a 1800 pound bell for the congregation for installation on the bell tower.

German Reformed Church

German immigrants migrating into the Aurora area formed the German Reformed Church in 1874, the congregation first began meeting in the Presbyterian church's basement.

Having outgrown the church on Fifth Street, the Baptists sold the building to the congregation of the German Reformed Church on June 12, 1875 and moved into a new, larger church on Main Street. A fire destroyed that church in 1928, burning many of the records of the earlier church.

First Evangelical United Church of Christ

The congregation has changed names as the years passed. The names included:

Erste Deutsche Evangeliche Protestantiche Kirche (Prior to 1916)

First German Evangelical Protestant Church of Aurora (1916)

First Evangelical Church (1924)

First Evangelical and Reformed Church (1934)

First Evangelical United Church of Christ (1957)

A major renovation of the church occurred in 1911. This involved removing the bell tower, replacing it with a steeple, removing the balcony, changing the front door to a single door instead of two and adding two stained glass windows. The congregation purchased a new organ in 1921, which was rebuilt in 1946. During the 1937 flood the Ohio River did not inundate the church, which served as a hospital. Congregation members staffed the hospital until Red Cross representatives arrived.

Moore's Hill United Methodist Church

Listed on the National Register of Historic Places

December 15, 1997

Reference # 97001537

Beginning in 1818 Methodists in Sparta Township began gathering for meetings at the home of Moses Musgrove. A circuit rider conducted services outside in warm weather and in a home during bad weather. That same year settlers in the area built a road that connected the township with Aurora. This road passed through the current site of Moore's Hill. Sometime in 1820 these early settler, mostly Methodist from Maryland and Delaware, began to meet at the home of John Dashiel, who lived nearby. Later they met at Adam Moore's home. In 1829 these Methodists constructed a small stone church on Moore's land. With the construction of the church and the convenience of the road, businesses began springing up. Moore's son, John, established a harness shop. The congregation built a new church in 1839 as it continued to grow. By 1851 the church acquired its first permanent minister. The congregation established Moore's Hill College in 1856. Since all the teachers and administrators were required to live in the town, the population grew. For more on the college, see its listing. The congregation constructed the current one story, brick in 1871, embellishing the simple structure with Greek Revival and Italianate details..

Moore's Hill United Methodist Church

13476 Main Street

Moore's Hill IN 47032

St. John's Lutheran Church and School

Local Lutherans established a congregation in Aurora in 1860. The congregation constructed the brick Gothic Revival structure in 1874. The structure was constructed by Aurora contractor William Barker. The church added several buildings on adjacent lots over the years. In 1954 the school house currently in use was added.

St. John's Lutheran Church and School

220 Mechanic Street

Aurora, IN 47001

(812) 926-3337

https://www.facebook.com/StJohnAurora/

State Line Archeological District

Listed on the National Register of Historic Places

July 24, 1975

Reference # 75001423

Located on the Indiana/Ohio state lines at the intersection of US Route 50 and State Line Road, the eight acre site is the scene of an active archeological study by an archaeological consulting firm, the ASC Group, Inc. The firm is working to document the site, as it is on the route of a planned intersection improvement project conducted by the Indiana Department of Transportation. The archeologists on site believe it was a village site populated by prehistoric native tribe. They have recovered pottery fragments, bone, weapons and stone tools.

Levi Stevens House

Listed on the National Register of Historic Places

May 30, 1996

Reference # 96000599

Constructed in 1849 for Levi E. Stevens, the 2 1/2 story house is of Greek Revival style of architecture. Mr. Stevens worked as a clerk on a steamboat named the "Fashion," owned by Josiah Chambers and William Glenn. He was also a partner in J. Chambers and Company. The home has changed hands many times over the year and has retained it original character.

Levi Stevens House

122 Fifth Street

Aurora, IN

Carnegie Hall

Listed on the National Register of Historic Places

March 17, 1994

Reference # 94000229

Visitors to Carnegie Hall in Moore's Hill, Indiana will find a unique structure with a unique history involving one of Indiana's, and probably the United States', earliest colleges to admit women.

Moore's Hill Male and Female Collegiate Institute

Established in 1854 by members of the Methodist Church, the Moore's Hill Male and Female Collegiate Institute was one of only two colleges in Indiana that admitted women. Built on land donated by Moore's Hill founder John Collins Moore, the original building, Moore Hall, stood on the western border of Dearborn County. The college received its charter in 1854 and opened by September 9, 1856. The school served students from first grade level through the baccalaureate level. An academy/preparatory department covered high school subjects and after 1871, the course study included a "normal school," that offered teacher training. College level classes included studies of the classics, music, art, and science. Later on the school taught classes in agriculture and commercial courses. The first graduate in 1858 was Miss Jane S. Churchill. The school changed its name to Moore's Hill College in 1887. Moore's Hall was a three-story building that became the dormitory for students after Carnegie Hall opened in 1908.

Carnegie Hall

The Crapsey and Lamm architectural firm of Cincinnati designed the two and a half story limestone Collegiate Gothic-Jacobethan Revival building with raised basement. The college by 1905 had outgrown Moore's Hall. The college's new president, Dr. Frank Clare English appealed to famous industrialist Andrew Carnegie to donate funds for a new building. Carnegie agreed to grant the college $18,750, which was half the proposed cost of $37,500 to build the new building. The fund raising effort was successful and on June 12, 1907, workers laid the cornerstone of the building. Work on the new building was completed on June 18, 1908 and named Carnegie Hall after Andrew Carnegie. Moore's Hall became the dormitory for students attending Moore's Hill College.

Demise

Moore's Hill College had funding problems. On November 4, 1915, Moore's Hall burned down. The college could not afford to build a new dormitory, thus the decision was made to move the college to Evansville, Indiana, which had raised $500,000 to get the college. Thus, in 1917 the college moved to Evansville and became Evansville College on February 17, 1919. Most historians consider Evansville College a continuation of Moore's Hill College and not a new college. Carnegie Hall found use as Moore's Hill High School until the school closed in 1968.

Restoration

Visitors to Carnegie Hall will find a restoration project under way as it strives for its official opening in April 2018. The museum features a wonderful museum on the first floor chronicling its days when it served as Moore's Hill High

School. Another room houses an early selection of early typewriters. The Carnegie Hall Auditorium is useful for live performances, music concerts and other events suitable for a small venue. Plans include using the basement, which has a large kitchen, as a site for receptions, reunions and other events. The dedicated volunteers of the Carnegie Historic Landmarks organization are working hard to restore the building and plan more additions to this wonderful building. Interested visitors can have a guided tour of the building by contacting the phone number listed below. A visit to this unique building is well worth the time spent.

Current plans are to open Carnegie Hall from 1:00 PM to 5:00 on Sunday, beginning in April 2018.

Carnegie Historic Landmarks

14687 Main Street

PO Box 118

Moore's Hill, IN 47032

(812) 744-4015

(812) 744-3493

www.thecarnegiehall.org/

Downtown Aurora Historic District

The Downtown Aurora Historic District includes a geographic area bounded by Hogan Creek to the north, the Ohio River to the east, the steep hill to the south and US 50 to the west. The area includes 274 contributing structures and 68 non-contributing.

Importing Street

Importing Street connects Eads Parkway with Judiciary Street, running along Hogan Creek just before it empties into the Ohio River. It intersects, from west to east, Bridgeway Street, Mechanic Street, Main Street/George Street and Judiciary Street. George Street crosses Hogan Street on the Pratt Truss George Street Bridge.

Many of the older buildings on Importing street date from the mid-19th Century T. and J. W. Gaff & Co. Distillery.

T. and J. W. Gaff & Co. Distillery - 322-304 Importing Street

Thomas Gaff established a distillery upon his arrival in Aurora in 1843. The distillery, located on the banks of Hogan Creek just before it empties into the Ohio River by 1850 had become one of the largest distilleries in the United States and produced bourbon, rye, and Thistle Dew scotch whiskey. Gaff had come at the invitation of Aurora's political leaders who offered tax incentives to the Gaff family if they would move their existing distillery business from Pennsylvania to Aurora. The location, right on the Ohio River, offered a convenient and necessary means of shipping their whiskey to markets across the United States.

Second Street

Second Street runs parallel to Importing Street, connecting Eads Avenue with Judiciary Street. Historic buildings located on the street include:

Ullrich's Drugstore

Located in a brick Italianate style building at 301 Second Street Wilfred John Ullrich operated a drug store, beginning sometime after 1929.

Wilfrid John Ullrich (May 6, 1908 - June 8, 1977)

The son of son of William W., and Irene Schipper Ullrich, Wilfrid was native to Aurora, Indiana. He graduated from Notre Dame with a chemistry degree in 1929. He and Eleanor Irene Klimek married that same year. The couple would have six children. Ullrich operated the Ullrich Drug Store on Second Street in Aurora for many years. Active in civic affairs, served in the Indiana Senate from 1963 until he died in 1977. He is interred in River View Cemetery in Aurora.

Chamber, Stevens & Co. Dry Goods Store

Josiah Chambers and Levi A. Stevens founded the store located at 222 Second Street in 1840. The store sold dry goods, groceries, hats and caps. They also dealt in queensware, which was a fine, cream colored type of pottery. Dry goods consisted of textiles, ready-to-wear clothing and sundries, which are generally products dealing with personal hygiene. The Queen Anne style building underwent an extensive remodeling in 1900.

Aurora Public Library

Baltimore and Ohio Southwest Railroad Passenger Station

Constructed after the railroad came through Aurora in 1859, the Baltimore and Ohio Southwest Railroad Passenger Station has been restored and retains its original ticket window and double doors. The Depot serves as Aurora's Local History Library and contains a host of information about the early history of Aurora and genealogical records of local residents.

The Local History Library @ The Depot

510 Second Street

Aurora, IN 47001 United States

http://aurora.in.us/library-and-depot.html

International Order of Odd Fellows Building

The Odd Fellows constructed the three story Romanesque Revival architecture building in 1887. They used the building to replace their previous headquarters at 213 Judiciary Street, which they had constructed in 1848. The Lyric Theater occupied the second story of the structure.

Odd Fellows

Founded in Baltimore, Maryland in 1819, the Oddfellows began as a group that visited sick people. In the days before modern medicine, this was a hazardous thing to do, as many contagions readily spread from person to person. The Oddfellows also had a commitment to an honorable burial of its members and established cemeteries near their lodges as a place of repose for departed members. The Oddfellows sold cemetery lots to non-members and in many cases these cemeteries became the primary cemetery in the community. For more information on the Oddfellows, contact:

Independent Order of Odd Fellows

422 Trade Street

Winston-Salem, North Carolina 27101 USA

Phone: 800-235-8358

http://www.ioof.org

Leive, Parks and Stapp Opera House

Listed National Register of Historic Places

September 20, 1994

Reference # 94001120

Constructed in 1878 by a partnership between three men, William Leive, John A. Parks and David H. Stapp, the three story Leive, Parks and Stapp Opera House provided an early entertainment venue for citizens of Aurora. Local celebrations like high school graduations and political meetings took place in the theatre. Traveling minstrel shows, theatrical troupes and lectures also took place in the theatre. The Italianate style structure featured two retail store spaces on the first floor. The second story provided dressing rooms for the actors and actresses at the rear of the building and possibly storage space and meeting hall in the front. The theatre was on the top floor with an ample stage and seating area. Apparently the theatre was quite grand in its day, however modifications over the years have led to the loss of its ornate features and left it with a basketball floor installed in the 1920's.

William Leive (January 13, 1839 - March 10, 1910)

Native to Hanover, Germany, Lieve immigrated Cincinnati, Ohio in 1852 with his parents when he was 13. The family moved into the Aurora region some time after that. William returned to Cincinnati to become an apprentice to a watchmaker named Milburn. By 1861 he returned to Aurora to open his own watchmaking business, apparently in the old Opera House. He married a lady named Reising from Cincinnati with whom he had three children. He maintained this business, which included selling watches, jewelry, books, pianos and organs, successfully for many years, teaching his son the business beginning in 1889. Lieve passed away in Aurora in 1910.

John A. Parks (August 18, 1850 - ?)

History has recorded little of Mr. Parks other than that he was the son of John G. and Yliva Bruce and that he was native to Hogan Township in Dearborn County. Apparently he studied law, received admittance to the bar and lived a prosperous life.

David H. Stapp (August 29, 1849 - August 2, 1917)

The son of Joseph and Indiana Watts Stapp, David was native to Dearborn County, Indiana. Stapp graduated from Hanover College in Madison in 1872. He gained admittance to the Indiana bar in 1874 and opened a practice in Aurora. During his time in Aurora he was instrumental in having several notable buildings around Aurora constructed. Stapp migrated to Chicago where he died on August 2, 1917. His remains were cremated in Chicago.

John Neff Building

John Neff (November 24, 1859 - January 5, 1935)

Native to Schneppenbach Germany, Neff immigrated to the United States sometime around 1880, settling in Aurora, Indiana sometime around 1885. Working at the trade of cobbler, he opened a shoe store with a man named Thomas Nees as partner. Nees left Aurora, after which Neff partnered with Frank Schipper. Neff made the shoes and took over full operations of the shop by 1893. Schipper opened his own business on Second Street after that. Neff relocated his store to the location on Second Street sometime during this decade. The same year he and Margaret Frankman married. The couple would have three daughters and seven sons. Five of the sons learned the shoe selling business. Two of the sons, Frank and George, took over the store in 1935. The store remained in business until 2015.

Third Street

United States Post Office

Constructed in 1935, the Aurora Post Office occupies the one-story, brown brick Georgian Revival structure at 511 Third Street. Indianapolis artist, Henrik Martin Mayer painted the mural in 1938. Entitled "Down to the Ferry," the project was part the Small New Deal program.

Dr. George Sutton Office

Dr. Sutton had this brick Second Empire structure constructed around 1870 to house his medical practice. He and his sons used the building for this purpose until 1921.

George Sutton (June 16, 1812 - June 13, 1886)

The son of George and Elizabeth Ives Sutton, George was native to London, England. In 1819 the family immigrated to the United States, living first in Cincinnati, then migrating to Franklin County. Sutton attended Miami University after which he enrolled at the Medical College of Ohio. After his graduation in 1836 he opened a practice in Aurora, Indiana. Beginning in 1843 Dr. Sutton began publishing papers he had written on the erysipelas epidemic, which is a bacterial infection of the skin which can cause a red rash and shivering, fever, headaches and vomiting. Commonly called Black Tongue, there was a widespread outbreak in Aurora and the surrounding countryside at the time. Dr. Sutton made good use of the microscope, using the tool to make valuable discoveries in trichina and the parasitic roundworms that caused the disease infected between three and that the ten percent of the hogs in southeastern Indiana. Consuming undercooked pork can cause infections in humans. He discovered that the infection created symptoms in humans that doctors had not known before. He also developed a new surgical means of correcting dislocations of the hip joint. Medical journals across the United States and the world published his papers. His studies led him to believe the origin of cholera, a disease killed one of his sons and made another extremely sick. His expertise led the Indiana State Medical Society to elect him president in 1867. He served as the seventh mayor of Aurora from 1863 - 1867. Doctor Sutton and his wife Sarah had five children. After his death, Dr. Sutton was interred at River View Cemetery in Aurora.

First United Methodist Church

Aurora Methodist Episcopal Church

Listed September 8, 1994

Reference # 94001113

Probably designed by local architect William Alien, this mid-19th century Greek Revival ecclesiastic architecture church was constructed between the years of 1855 and 1862.

Tandy's Grocery Store

Erected in 1969, this brick building occupies somewhat over half of the block between Third, Judiciary and Main Streets.

Washington/Union/St. Clair Hotel

Constructed by John Nees in 1877, the two story brick Italianate building served as a hotel, grocery store and fresh produce market.

John Nees (November 2, 1830 - October 9, 1901)

The son of Thomas and Eva (Parr) Nees, John was native to Bayern, Germany. As a child he worked on his father's farm in Germany and received his education at the common schools there. Posing as the son of the Wolbert family to gain passage across the Atlantic, he migrated to the United States in 1847. He worked as a cooper in Cincinnati, Ohio for two years until a cholera outbreak led him to move to New Richmond, Ohio. In New Richmond he taught at a Catholic school and performed as a church organist. After a few years he migrated to Aurora, Indiana, arriving on August 27, 1867. He became involved in the grocery, hotel and saloon business from the beginning. He constructed the 27 room Washington/Union/St. Clair Hotel in 1877 at a cost of $10,000. In 1852 he and Amelia Koch married. The couple would have 15 children. Mr. Nees was one of the organizers of St. Mary's Church. After his death in 1901 he was interred at River View Cemetery. Plot # 3086.

Fourth Street

At somewhat less than a mile long. Fourth Street runs from its intersection with Indiana State Road 56 in downtown Aurora to its terminus at its second intersection with Conwell Street on the southwestern edge of Aurora. Primarily residential, Fourth Street does have several structures that are historically noteworthy.

David and Jennie Stapp Residence

306 Fourth Street,

Constructed around 1883 for David and Jennie Stapp, the 2 1/2 story Italianate style house incorporates Italianate and Moorish Revival elements. The Stapps sold the house in 1891.

First Presbyterian Church

Listed on the National Register of Historic Places

September 08, 1994

Reference # 94001116

The Reverend Lucius Alden laid the foundations of the current First Presbyterian Church in 1826. Representing the American Home Missionary

Society, Reverend Alden established a Presbyterian seminary in Aurora. This establishment lasted only until 1828.

First Presbyterian Church

Reverend Windsor A. Smith, who was the pastor of the Presbyterian church in Lawrenceburg, established a congregation in Aurora in 1844. The ten initial members began meeting without the benefit of a church building, however in in 1848 the growing church acquired the land the church now stands on. By December 8, 1850 the construction on the first floor had completed and members began holding services there. Cincinnati architect John R. Hamilton designed the mid-nineteenth century Greek Revival religious structure church, which was completed in 1855. The church acquired its first pipe organ, which many believe to be the first one in Dearborn County, in 1860 after a steamboat carrying it wrecked near the town. The congregation used this organ until replacing it in 1905. During these years rumors circulated that it was part of the Underground Railroad system, however the church kept no records of the activity. This was not uncommon, as harboring runaway slaves was a crime and could bring fines and imprisonment on individuals involved.

St. Mary's Catholic Church and School

By 1848 the Catholic population of Aurora had reached about 700, however they had no church to serve their needs. A popular notary, I.E. Labrie, traveled to Bourbonnais, Illinois to converse with the parish priest there about establishing a Catholic Church in Aurora. In February 1849 the Reverend Courjeault traveled from Bourbonnais to Aurora to administer Mass to Aurora's Catholics in the schoolhouse during a three-day mission. This schoolhouse stood in what is now Lincoln Park. Father Louis A. Courjeault visited Aurora and persuaded the second Bishop of Chicago James O. Vandevelde to come to Aurora in September 1850. The Bishop returned in 1851 to purchase 19.5 acres of land on which to establish a church, called the Sacred Heart. He purchased the land on February 10, 1851 and construction of 75 X 40 feet chapel commenced almost immediately. A destructive windstorm struck on December 24, 1852, causing a great amount of damage to this church. The Church sold this property to the railroad and purchased another tract at the intersection Pine and Spruce Streets and built a second church, also called Sacred Heart. A fire destroyed this church on November 8, 1869. Again, the Church sold the property and purchased the tract where the current church now stands. The dedication for this church, renamed the name to St. Mary's, occurred in July 1872. The school was added in 1902, staffed with nuns from the Sisters of Providence from St.-Mary-of-the-Woods near Terra Haute.

St. Mary's Parish + School

203 4th Street

Aurora, IN 47001

(812) 926-0060

https://mystmarys.com/

Downtown Lawrenceburg Historic District

Listed on the National Register of Historic Places

March 1, 1984

Reference # 84001009

Geographic Area

The area included in the Historic District is about three and a half blocks long and five blocks wide with about 300 contributing structures. The District encompasses almost the entire area contained in the original 1803 plat of the city created by Samuel Vance. The boundaries of the district are approximately Tate Street on the northwest, High Street on the southeast, Charlotte Street on the southwest and Short Street on the northeast.

Buildings of Historic Interest

Lawrenceburg Public Library;

Classical Revival/Modern, 1915/1959 (C)

Lawrenceburg Public Library District

Lawrenceburg residents circulated and signed a petition for a public library which led to the establishment of the Lawrenceburg Public Library's opening on May 18, 1910. Miss Elizabeth Kirtley served as the first librarian. The library's first location was in the old Post Office Building on Short Street. The library had a total of 2000 books. The State of Indiana donated 1400 books with the remainder coming as gifts from local residents. The Library was open three days a week, Tuesday, Thursday and Saturday. Daytime hours were 1:00 - 5:00 PM and evening hours were 7:00 PM to 9:00 PM on Tuesday and Saturday.

Miss Ada Fitch became the second librarian in 1911. The Great Flood of 1913, which occurred from March 23 - 26,

77

closed the library for eleven days. In 1914 Miller Township, which includes Guilford and Bright, joined the District.

New Library

The library received a Carnegie Grant the same year. Mr. and Mrs. Victor Oberting donated a partial lot on High Street for a new library, with the City of Lawrenceburg donating the rest. The Obertings and the City donated an additional $800.00. The Lawrenceburg Public Library District held its dedication ceremony on October 19, 1915. The new library was constructed thirteen inches above the 1913 flood line and measured 58 feet long and 36 feet wide. A basement auditorium held 250 people. The book collection had grown to 4,000 books. The library established a Book Wagon service in 1920 and hired Miss Corinne Tebbs as head librarian. Her assistant was Miss Boyd.

1937 Flood

From January 13 through January 25 record levels of rainfall fell in Ohio. The rainwater poured into the Ohio River where rising flood waters crated record floods over the Ohio River Valley region. The rising waters breached the Lawrenceburg levee. The waters rose to 82 feet 6 inches in Lawrenceburg, inundating the entire city. The city remained flooded for two weeks. The flood destroyed the entire collection in the Lawrenceburg Library, which did not reopen until September 1, 1937.

Later Renovations

A major renovation took place in 1958 in which the basement was filled in, the steps removed and a new glass front added to the building. The Library District purchased an adjoining law office to expand the growing library. A 1987 renovation to the original Carnegie building resulted in an additional 10,000 square feet. The new sections included a children's section and a genealogical department.

New Library

A $1.4 million bond issue and funds from the Library Improvement Fund led to the construction of a new library, dedicated on May 22, 1988. This library was located at 123 West High Street.

Five Dearborn County townships, Harrison, Kelso, Logan and York, joined the Lawrenceburg Public Library District in 1995. The remaining counties joined the Aurora district.

The District purchased a Bookmobile from the Bedford Public Library and established Mobile Outreach Library Service in 2002.

In September 2005 the City of Lawrenceburg and the Library Board of Trustees approved a $6,316.824 building project for a new library. A ground breaking ceremony took place on July 2006 with the dedication for the new library taking place on September 9, 2007. In 2017 the District purchased a new mobile library vehicle.

Lawrenceburg Public Library District

150 Mary Street

Lawrenceburg, IN 47025

Lawrenceburg Public Library District

https://www.lpld.lib.in.us

lawplib@lpld.lib.in.us

Lawrenceburg Depot

Constructed about 1885, the Queen Anne style Lawrenceburg Train Depot is located on West William Street. The depot currently serves as an annex for the Lawrenceburg Library.

Jesse Hunt House; Federal

An historical maker located on the building notes:

1812 • Jacob Horner buys lot #157, builds log tavern on corner.

1817 • Jesse Hunt leases Horner's Tavern.

1818 • Hunt purchases and removes log tavern.

1819 • Hunt builds first 3-story brick building in Indiana, Benj. Stockman, brick mason. Livestock drovers enter tavern through cellar.

c.1825 • Hunt buys lot #158; 3-story additions to east & south. Hunt House operates over 50 years.

c.1885 • Known as Grand Hotel; remodeled after floods of 1882-83-84, pressed metal cornice added.

c.1900 • Operating as Anderson House.

c.1920 • Perry A. Kind operates King Hotel until 70's. Bedford stone facing added c.1960.

1988 • Hunts Tavern restaurant closes. Hotel vacant, for sale.

1993 • T.J.R. Contractors Inc. Guts interior for senior housing. Riverboat gaming approved for Lawrenceburg.

1994 • Golden Nugget buys hotel and three blocks on south side of High Street.

1998 • Demolition permit issued: lawsuit prevents demolition.

1999 • Historic Landmarks Foundation of Indiana buys hotel and 13 other buildings downtown.

2000 • Facade restoration and stabilization

Hunt House Hotel Marker image. Click for full size.

By Ginger Drenning, August 23, 2009

2. Hunt House Hotel Marker

The marker is the one on the left in the photo.

completed.

2003 • United Community Bank buys hotel and begins restoration.

2004 • United Community Bank opens Corporate Headquarters and branch operation.

Marker placed by:

Historic Lawrenceburg, Greendale Foundation

Jesse Hunt House

6 East High Street

Lawrenceburg, IN 47025

McCullough Drug Building

High Street

Build around 1865 the Federal style building became the home of the McCullough Drug Building in 1874 when John C. McCullough relocated to Lawrenceburg.

John C. McCullough (1850 - 1906)

The son of John and Agnes McCullough was native to Washington County, Pennsylvania. McCullough's family immigrated to Morrow County, Ohio around 1855. He attended Central College in Iberia, Ohio, after which he moved to Osgood, Indiana in 1867. In Osgood, he opened a drug wholesale business. In 1872 he and Louisa Koon married. the couple would have three children. He moved the business to Newtown, in Lawrenceburg, Indiana in 1874. In 1888 he received appointment as a revenue collector for the Federal Government, a position he held until 1891 when poor health forced him to resign. he moved to Warsaw,

Indiana to open to open another drug business, however after a year he returned to Lawrenceburg to return to the drug wholesaling business in Oldtown. He sold that business and began a business manufacturing drugs. He and his son John received several patents for the drugs they devised. They incorporated the business in 1901. The company went out of business after the 1937 flood caused extensive damage to the building.

Knights of Pythias Lodge

Italianate, c.1870 (C)

Lawrenceburg Lodge # 49

Established on July 2, 1874, the lodge began with 13 members. Around 1870 the Lodge built the three story building, renting the first story out to other businesses, the second story as a club room and the third story as the meeting room. The second story included a kitchen and waiting room.

Knights of Pythias

Founded by Justus H. Rathbone in Washington, DC on Feb 19, 1864, the Knights of Pythias is a non-sectarian fraternal organization. The Order has chapters, called Domains, in most states across the United States. The Order uses the story of Damon and Pythias, who lived at the beginning of the Christian era, to base its lessons and rituals. Damon and Pythias were friends. The king of Syracuse had gained the throne by fraud. Damon had opposed him. The king condemned Damon to death. Pythias stood as a hostage to Damon when he journeyed home to bid farewell to his family and friends. The story engenders the loyalty the two friends displayed by their willingness to die for each other. Justus H. Rathbone had seen a play, written by Irish poet John Banim about the story. The performance led him to found an order that members would vow to duplicate this friendship with other members. For more information, contact:

Knights of Pythias

http://www.pythias.org

Klausing's Packard Garage; Art

Art-Deco style building constructed around 1930.

Klausing's Packard Garage

345 Walnut Street

Lawrenceburg, IN 47025

Carpenters Union Meeting Hall

The Carpenter's Union Meeting Hall was constructed around 1860.

117 Short Street

Lawrenceburg, IN 47025

Beecher Presbyterian Church

Established by Samuel Bainbridge in 1803, the Presbyterian Church in Lawrenceburg officially organized on September 28, 1829. The congregation built their first church in 1831. This church's served as a school room. It would later be the home of Lawrenceburg High School. The congregation built the parsonage in 1846. The congregation had the original church razed in 1882, after which they constructed the current church occupying the site. Up until the decade of the 1920's the church was called the First Presbyterian Church.

Sometime during that time it was changed to Beecher Presbyterian Church.

Queen Anne, 1882 (O)

Beecher Presbyterian Church

229 Short Street

Lawrenceburg, IN 47025

https://beecherpresbyterianchurch.weebly.com/

Dearborn County - Museums

Carnegie Hall

Carnegie Historic Landmarks

14687 Main Street

PO Box 118

Moore's Hill, IN 47032

(812) 744-4015

(812) 744-3493

For more information, see the listing in the National Register of Historic Places section

www.thecarnegiehall.org/

Dearborn County Historical Society

Located in the historic Vance-Tousey House in downtown Lawrenceburg, the Dearborn County Historical Society offers a variety of services for visitors interested in the county's rich history, including genealogical research assistance, the restored Angevine Log Cabin and programs and special events on occasion. It is a must place to visit to learn the history of this part of southeast Indiana.

Vance-Tousey House

Constructed by Lawrenceburg founder Samuel C. Vance, this 1818 structure is a two-story, five bay, Late Georgian / Federal style brick and sandstone home. The National Register of Historic Places listed it in 2000. Omer Tousey owned the home later on.

Angevine Log Cabin

Built by James Angevine around 1820 to replace an earlier cabin that a flooding Tanners Creek washed away. Native to New York City, Angevine had been a sailor before moving to Dearborn County in 1818, where he opened a grocery store. He and his wife Susan raised twelve children in this cabin. They lived in the cabin untl 1834 when they built a bigger brick home higher up on the hill. The Dearborn County Historical Society purchased, moved and restored the cabin in 1985.

Dearborn County Historical Society

508 West High Street

Lawrenceburg, IN 47025

http://www.rootsweb.ancestry.com/~indbchs/

deahistory@embarqmail.com

Hillforest

213 Fifth Street

P.O. Box 127

Aurora, IN 47001

http://www.hillforest.org

hillforest@embarqmail.com

Veraestau Historic Site

Indiana Landmarks Southeast Field Office

4696 Veraestau Lane

Aurora, IN 47001-9406

812-926-0983

https://www.facebook.com/Veraestau/

veraestau@indianalandmarks.org

Dearborn County Historical Markers

Dearborn Historical Marker — Guilford Covered Bridge

Guilford Covered Bridge

Inscription. Built 1879

Original Design by Archibald M. Kennedy and Sons

Additional Structural Supports added in the early 1900s to sustain heavier loads produced by Guilford's rail commerce

Moved from Yorkridge Rd to park in 1960

Damaged by fire in 1993

Restored in 1997 by LL Brown Co. and the Amos Schwartz Co

For the Dearborn County Park and Recreation Board

And the Dearborn County Commissioners

Location. 39° 10.215' N, 84° 54.508' W.

Marker is in Guilford, Indiana, in Dearborn County.

Marker can be reached from Main Street.

Marker is inside the bridge on the right side as you pass under the bridge from the road.

The Bridge is located in the Guilford Covered Bridge Park.

Marker is at or near this postal address:

4785 Main Street, Guilford IN 47022, United States of America.

Brief History by the Author
Guilford Covered Bridge

Guilford has the last remaining covered bridge in Dearborn County, constructed by noted bridge builder Archibald M. Kennedy & Sons of Rushville. Mr. Kennedy was hired by the County Commissioners in 1879 to construct the 101-foot long bridge spanning East Fork Tanners Creek. Because the bridge was to be torn down and replaced by a concrete bridge in 1961 the people of the county banded together to save the old structure. The populace of Guilford raised the funds needed to tear it down and move it to its current location, in the Guilford Covered Bridge Park, at the intersection of Indiana State Road 1 and York Ridge Road. An arsonist damaged the bridge in 1993; locals restored the bridge in 1997. Visitors to the park drive through the bridge as they enter the park.

Archibald Kennedy (August 25, 1818 - June 3, 1897)

A native of Guilford County, North Carolina, he was the son of E. L. Kennedy and Martha Kennedy. The family moved to Fayette County, Indiana in 1818. He started working as a carpenter in 1841 and started building covered bridges as a side business in 1853. His first bridge was a two span bridge over the east fork of the Whitewater River in Franklin County. Archibald showed prowess as a bridge builder and this soon became his chief occupation. He passed the bridge building business on to his sons who in turn passed it on to their sons. The family bridge building business lasted three generations and during that time, they built at least fifty-eight bridges.

Approximate latitude, longitude

+39.17017, -84.90867   (decimal degrees)

39°10'13" N, 84°54'31" W   (degrees°minutes'seconds")

Approximate UTM coordinates

16/680665/4337743 (zone/easting/northing)

Bridgehunter.com ID 16006

Dearborn Historical Marker East Fork Stone Chapel

East Fork Stone Chapel

By Tom Bosse, July 18, 2015

Inscription.

Erected 1821 by early settlers as a Methodist Church on land donated by John Ewbank. Services were held continuously for more than 125 years. Maintained by endowment fund.

Erected 1966 by Dearborn County Sesquicentennial Committee.

Location. 39° 11.327' N, 84° 54.244' W.

Marker is in Guilford, Indiana, in Dearborn County.

Marker is on Indiana Route 1 0.1 miles south of E. Fork Road, on the left when traveling north.

Marker is in this post office area: Guilford IN 47022, United States of America.

Brief History by the Author

Parishioners used rock from nearby Tanner's Creek to construct this church in 1821. Members held services in the church for 125 years, until the 1940's. John Ewbank lived in the area and used the cemetery as a family plot. The Ewbank family donated the cemetery and the land for the church, thus visitors will find graves older than 1821. The marker is visible from Indiana State Road 1. To access the church go to East Fork Road and turn left, if coming from Lawrenceburg. The cemetery and graveyard are on the west side of the road. East Fork Road loops back to State Road 1, so turning around are not necessary.

Dearborn Historical Marker - The Price of Freedom

The Price of Freedom Marker image..

By Ginger Drenning, August 23, 2009

Inscription.

THE PRICE OF FREEDOM

Dedicated in Honor of All men and women who have served in the Armed Forces and Sacrificed Unselfishly for the Freedom of the United States of America

(Left - Memorial)

Serving those who served

(Seals of ::)

American Legion

Disabled American Veterans

Vietnam Veterans of America

(Right - Memorial)

Serving those who served

(Seals of ::)

Veterans of Foreign Wars

AMVETS - American Veterans of World War II

40 / 8

(Starting from the Left of the Entire Memorial)

(First - Memorial)

REVOLUTIONARY WAR

Apr. 19, 1775 - - - Sept. 3, 1783

4,435 - Lives Lost

WAR OF 1812

June 18, 1812 - - - Jan. 8, 1815

2,260 - Lives Lost

MEXICAN WAR

May 13, 1846 - - - Feb. 2, 1848

13,283 - Lives Lost

CIVIL WAR

Apr. 12, 1861 - May 26, 1865

620,000 - Lives Lost

(Second - Memorial)

SPANISH AMERICAN WAR

Apr. 25, 1898 - Dec. 10, 1898

2,446 - Lives Lost

World War I

Apr. 6, 1917

By Ginger Drenning, August 23, 2009

2. Center Left - - The Price of Freedom Marker

- Nov. 11, 1918

116,516 - Lives Lost

World War II

Dec. 7, 1941 - Dec. 31, 1946

405,399 - Lives Lost

KOREAN WAR

June 25, 1950 - July 27, 1953

54,246 - Lives Lost

(Third - Memorial)

Angels

of Mercy

(Fourth - Memorial)

AIR FORCE

Est. Aug. 1, 1907

Activity in the air began with the use of balloons by the Army for reconnaissance. The first aircraft in action was in 1916 against Pancho Villa in Mexico. On July 26, 1947 the National Security Act created the independent U. S. Air Force.

""OFF WE GO INTO THE WILD BLUE YONDER""

(Fifth - Memorial)

MARINES

Est. Nov. 10, 1775

A proud group that fights in the air, on land and sea. They assault enemy held beaches. Securing the position for other forces, and guard our American Embassies. They have fought in all conflicts and proclaim that they are the "First to Fight for Right and Freedom"

""SEMPER FIDELIS - ALWAYS FAITHFUL""

(Sixth - Memorial)

ARMY

Est. June 14, 1775

The first organized defense for the budding United States, and today still defends God, Liberty, and Country. It's equipped with the most modern weapons systems in the World, with troops that can be moved quickly to any global location where our interests are threatened.

""THIS WE'LL DEFEND""

(Past Center Section)
(First - Memorial)
COAST GUARD
Est. Aug. 4, 1790

Formed to guard the coasts against smugglers. They police shorelines and harbors, enforce navigation regulations, and conduct searches from water and air for people lost at sea. They maintain transmitting stations that send navigation signals all over the World.
""SEMPER PARATUS - ALWAYS READY""

(Second - Memorial)
NAVY
Est. Oct. 13, 1775

It controls the waters by defeating attacks in the air and on the sea. It also transports troops, equipment, and supplies. They have pioneered nuclear powered guided missiles. Superior technology makes our navy the most feared in the World.
""ANCHORS AWAY""

(Third - Memorial)
MERCHANT MARINES
Est. 1775

The American colonies' merchant fleet had the most ships destroyed during the Revolutionary War. Ship numbers increased during the 1800's, WW I and WW II. The cargo they carry aids greatly in defeating the enemy. Ship types are dry-cargo and tankers, as well as passenger.

""IN PEACE AND WAR""

(Fourth - Memorial)

The Supreme

Sacrifice

(Fifth - Memorial)

VIETNAM WAR

Aug. 4, 1964 - Jan. 27, 1973

58,167 - Lives Lost

GRENADA

Oct. 25, 1983 - Nov. 2, 1983

19 - Lives Lost

PANAMA

Dec. 20, 1989 - Jan. 31, 1990

23 - Lives Lost

DESERT SHIELD / STORM

Aug. 7, 1990 - Apr. 1, 1991

390 - Lives Lost

(Sixth - Memorial)

SOMALIA

Dec. 9, 1992 - Mar. 28, 1994

44 - Lives Lost

(Back of Entire Memorial)

(First Right - Memorial)

The Veterans Memorial Committee

expresses appreciation to the

Dearborn County Government

for their approval and support of

this monument on June 3, 1991

COMMISSIONERS

R. Rodney Dennerline, Pres.

Robert A. Hoffmeier

Barrott H. Nanz

COUNCIL

James B. Wismann, Pres.

Vera Benning

Larry W. Givan

Kathy S. Klump

Dennis A. Kraus

George (Bo) Lansing

Randall J. Lyness

ADMINISTRATOR
Louis J. Meyer

ATTORNEY
William K. Ewan

AUDITOR
Jackie Stutz
(
First Left Memorial - - The Price of Freedom Marker image.
By Ginger Drenning, August 23, 2009
5. First Left Memorial - - The Price of Freedom Marker
Second Right - Memorial)
" Veteran's Memorial Committee "
CHAIRPERSON
Patricia Fox

VICE CHAIRMAN
Herbert Poole

SECRETARY
Melba Earles

TREASURER

Della Holliday

MEMBERS

Robert Hedrick

Clarence Batchelor

Ken Hylton

Glynn Clark

Joe Koch

Al Werner

Ronald Woodward

Mike Klump

Paul McKinley

Dorothea McKinley

Donald Earles

Red Childers

Edwin Powell

Carroll E. Ammons

Marcus Holliday

Annie Werner

Erected 1994 by Veteran's Memorial Committee.

Location. 39° 5.482' N, 84° 50.991' W.

Marker is in Lawrenceburg, Indiana, in Dearborn County.

Marker is on Mary Street north of West High Street, on the left when traveling north.

Located on the South/East lawn of the Dearborn County Courthouse in Lawrenceburg, Indiana.

Marker is at or near this postal address: 215 West High Street, Lawrenceburg IN 47025, United States of America.

Dearborn County Historical Marker - Dearborn County World War I War Memorial

Dearborn County World War I War Memorial

http://www.hmdb.org/marker.asp?marker=22203

By Ginger Drenning, August 23, 2009

Inscription.

Honor Roll

In Grateful remembrance of the boys of Dearborn County who gave their lives in the World War 1917 - 1918.

Erected by the Citizens of Dearborn County, Indiana

Walter Ahrens • Henry Fred Amm • Elmer Andrews • Hobart S. Bailey • Harry Bales • Louis A. Bartels • Raymond F. Beard • Floyd Becker • Charles H. Bildner • John V. Bildner • John R. Boyd • Bernard H. Burke • Harvey J. Clarke • Millard Dennerline • Edwin F. Engelking • Edwin M. Fox • William J. Haske • Dewey H. Hauck • Otto G. Hammerle • George Henry Johnson • Ervin H. Laaker • David H. McCallister • Thomas Miles • Michael George Miller • Julius J. Miller • Stanley Northcutt • Charles E. Orsborn • Albinus L. Ratz • William Keith Ross • Harvey H. Rusche • Charles Lloyd Singer • Howard Slayback • Halstead F. Scott • Henry F. Scharf • Frederick C. Steele • Russell Winkley • Earl White • Roy Lee White

Erected by Citizens of Dearborn County.

Location. 39° 5.46' N, 84° 50.989' W. Marker is in Lawrenceburg, Indiana, in Dearborn County.

Marker is on West High Street west of Mary Street, on the right when traveling west.

Located on the right pillar as you enter the front door (West Wide View - - World War I War Memorial Marker Photo

High Street) to the Dearborn County Courthouse in Lawrenceburg, Indiana.

Marker is at or near this postal address: 215 West High Street, Lawrenceburg IN 47025, United States of America.

Brief History by the Author

World War I (July 28, 1914 - November 11, 1918)

Known for many years as the Great War, World War I commenced when a Serbian nationalist, Gavrilo Princip, assassinated the Austro-Hungarian heir to the throne, Archduke Franz Ferdinand. The assassination occurred while the Archduke and his wife rode through the streets of Sarajevo, Bosnia in an open car. The assassination set off a chain of events that led to a protracted, disastrous war that lasted four long years. An estimated nine million soldiers died in the conflict, with another twenty million wounded. Historians estimate that over seven million civilians died in the conflict. Slavic Nationalism within the Austro-Hungarian Empire, entangling alliances and many other factors created what had been to that date the most destructive war in European history.

Austro-Hungarian Empire

Known by many names, the most common being Austria-Hungary, the Empire came into existence on March 30, 1867. The Empire consisted of a union between Austria, Hungary and the Kingdom of Croatia-Slavonia. It was an uneasy union; with the Slavic peoples of Serbia, Bosnia,

Herzegovina and Croatia each having their own national government and a nationalist movement that demanded complete independence. By 1914, ethnic tensions had risen to a fever pitch. The Emperor of Austria, Franz Joseph I, feared that the nationalism would rip his empire apart.

Entangling Alliances

The "Balance of Power" in Europe included two main alliances. These were the Triple Entente (Allies) and the Central Powers. The Allies consisted of England, France and Russian Empire. Germany and Austria-Hungary comprised the Central Powers. The Ottoman Empire would join the alliance after the war began.

War Begins

The Austria-Hungary government decided that it would end the nationalist movement after the assassination. After receiving assurances from Germany that it would support them, they delivered an ultimatum to the Serbian government. The Serbs accepted nine of the ten demands, but vacillated on the tenth. In retaliation, Austria-Hungary declared war on July 28, 1914. The Russian Empire supported the Serbs and mobilized its troops. Germany began a two front offensive, invading France through Belgium and Luxembourg, leading Great Britain to declare war against Germany in support of its allies. Germany then invaded Russia. By late summer, the consortium of nations at war grew.

United States Neutral

The United States maintained a policy of neutrality, but its inclinations were towards the Allies. Germany had declared a policy of unrestricted submarine warfare, a policy that included torpedoing passenger ships it suspected of carrying munitions from the United States to Great Britain. The United States demanded a halt to this, a demand to which eventually Germany acceded. The resumption of this policy and the interception of the Zimmerman Telegram changed all of this.

Zimmerman Telegram

The Germans suspected that the United States would eventually enter the war on the side of the Allies. German Foreign Minister Arthur Zimmermann sent a telegram to the Mexican government, inviting them to join the alliance and declare war against the United States in January 1917. British intelligence intercepted the telegram, deciphered it and gave it to United States' officials. An irate United States declared war against Germany on April 6, 1917. The United States was at war.

The United States in World War I

The war effort developed quickly. By summer 1917, the United States sent over ten thousand troops a day to Europe. In all, the nation would draft almost three million men for the war. The United States would suffer 116,516 casualties during the war, 53,402 in combat by the time the combatants signed an armistice on November 11, 1918.

Find more information and view archival photos of World War I at this link.

https://www.archives.gov/research/military/ww1/

Dearborn County Historical Marker - Dearborn County

Dearborn County

By Ginger Drenning, August 23, 2009

Inscription.

Formed by proclamation of Indiana Territorial Governor William Henry Harrison March 7, 1803. Named in honor of Major General Henry Dearborn, Secretary of War.

The third county to be formed, it was originally much larger. Its present boundaries were established January 7, 1845.

First courthouse built 1810, second built 1828, present limestone courthouse built 1870 - 1871.

Erected 1976 by Dearborn County Bicentennial Committee.

Location:

39° 5.462' N, 84° 50.988' W.

Marker is in Lawrenceburg, Indiana, in Dearborn County.

Marker is on West High Street south of Mary Street, on the right when traveling south.

Located at the South East corner of the Dearborn County Courthouse Lawn in Lawrenceburg, Indiana.

Marker is at or near this postal address:

215 West High Street, Lawrenceburg IN 47025, United States of America.

Brief History

See Dearborn County post

Dearborn County Historical Marker - Korean War Memorial

Dearborn County Korean War Memorial

By Ginger Drenning, August 23, 2009

Inscription.

KOREAN WAR

This plaque is dedicated in grateful remembrance of the men of Dearborn County who served their Country in the Korean War.

In God we trust

Erected by the Citizens of Dearborn County Indiana.

Location. 39° 5.458' N, 84° 50.991' W.

Marker is in Lawrenceburg, Indiana, in Dearborn County.

Marker is on West High Street west of Mary Street, on the right when traveling west.

located at the front entrance (on a pillar to the right) of the Dearborn County Courthouse in Lawrenceburg, Indiana.

Marker is at or near this postal address:

215 West High Street, Lawrenceburg IN 47025, United States of America.

Brief History by the Author

Korean War (June 25 - 1950)

The Korean War became the first armed major conflict during the post World War II Cold War.

Historical Background

Korea occupies a peninsula northwest of Japan on that divides the Sea of Japan, the Yellow Sea and the East China Sea. Japan had taken advantage of the turmoil created by the Russo-Japanese War and annexed Korea using the Japan-Korea Annexation Treaty in 1910. Japan continued its expansionist policy in the years leading up to World War II, when its attack on the United States Naval base on Pearl Harbor brought the United States into war with Japan. By the end of the war, the United States had allied itself with Great Britain, France and the Soviet Union in their united effort to defeat the Axis powers of Japan, Germany and Italy. In the closing days of the war, the United States and the Soviet Union had agreed to divide the country, with the border at the 38th Parallel. After the war tensions rose between the western capitalist, democratic nations with the Communist powers, China and the Soviet Union. US forces had occupied South Korea, which was developing into a democratic, capitalist nation. North Korea had adopted the Communist, authoritarian model of its larger mentors. In an attempt to conquer the south and bring it into Communist fold, 75,000 North Korean forces invaded the South on June 25, 1950. The United Nations called for a cease-fire, which the North Koreans ignored. Chinese and Soviet Union supported the North Korean drive to unite the country and almost succeeded. United States forces, already in the country, responded. The fighting continued until the two countries signed an armistice on July 27, 1953. The nations have maintained a tense relationship in the years since, with US Forces still maintaining a strong presence along the border.

United States Deaths Korean War

The United State suffered 33,686 combat casualties doing the three-year war. The United States had provided about 88% of the UN forces that resisted the invasion.

For more information about Korean War veterans and memorials, contact:

Korean War Veteran's Association

KWVA, PO Box 407

Charleston, IL 61920-0407

http://www.kwva.org/

Dearborn County Historical Marker - Lawrenceburg - Founded 1802

Lawrenceburg - Founded 1802

By Duane Hall, May 21, 2013

1. Lawrenceburg Marker

Inscription

Birthplace of two Indiana Governors. Albert Gallatin Porter, eighteenth Governor (1881-1885), born here April 20, 1824, died Indianapolis, May 3, 1897; and Winfield Taylor Durbin, twenty-fourth Governor (1901-1905), born here May 4, 1847, died Anderson, December 18, 1928.

Erected 1976 by Dearborn County Bicentennial Committee.

Marker series. This marker is included in the Spirit of 76, America's Bicentennial Celebration marker series.

http://www.historicalmarkerproject.com/series/177/the-spirit-of-76-americas-bicentennial-celebration.html

Location 39° 5.762' N, 84° 51.481' W.

Marker is in Lawrenceburg, Indiana, in Dearborn County.

Marker is at the intersection of Green Boulevard (U.S. 50) and Park Street, on the right when traveling east on Green Boulevard.

Marker is located in Lawrenceburg Newton Park fronting Green Blvd (US50).

Marker is in this post office area: Lawrenceburg IN 47025, United States of America.

Brief History by the Author

Albert Gallatin Porter (April 20, 1824 – May 3, 1897)

The son of Thomas and Myra Tousey Porter, Albert is native to Lawrenceburg, Indiana. The family farm's location on the banks of the Ohio River made it possible for Porter to earn his college money by tending his father's ferry. He attended Hanover College in Madison until his funds ran out. An uncle offered to pay his tuition if he attended a Methodist College, thus he attended and graduated from Asbury College in Wilmore, Kentucky. After completing college, he returned to Lawrenceburg to study law. A Democrat, he served as the private secretary to Governor James Whitcomb. Porter would marry Whitcomb's daughter, Minerva, on November 20, 1846. The couple would have five children.

Politics

During the time he served as the governor's secretary, Porter also worked as the reporter for the Indiana Supreme Court, writing for the Indianapolis Journal. The political chaos after the Kansas-Nebraska Act of 1854 allowed the expansion of slavery into United States territories. During the dissention in the Democratic Party between pro-slavery and anti-slavery factions, the pro-slavery people won. The party expunged many anti-slavery members, Porter among them. He joined the new Republican Party, gaining election to the United States House of Representatives in 1858 and 1860.

Private Practice

After his term expired in 1862, Porter returned to private life, working as a lawyer. President Rutherford P. Hayes appointed him as comptroller of the United States Treasury in 1877, a position he held until 1880.

Governor

The Republicans nominated him for governor in 1880, a post he won by a narrow margin. During his two terms, Porter was instrumental in establishing hospitals for the insane, the State Board of Health and introducing a drainage program for marshlands and the Great Kankakee Swamp in northwestern Indiana. This program added hundreds of agricultural acres to the state. He also advocated women's suffrage and helped institutive stricter mining regulations, which helped improve the working conditions for miners.

Out of Office

Porter remained active after his term expired, serving as a delegate to the 1888 Republican National Convention. As delegate, he delivered a speech nominating his old law partner and friend, Benjamin Harrison, for President. Harrison won and named Porter as Minister to Italy in 1889. He held this position until he resigned in 1892. He returned to Indianapolis and began collecting material for a History of Indiana. He died before finishing the task. The work remains unpublished. His remains are interred in Crown Hill Cemetery in Indianapolis.

Winfield Taylor Durbin (May 4, 1847 – December 18, 1928)

The son of William S. and Eliza Ann Sparks, Winfield was native to Lawrenceburg, Indiana. The family moved to New Philadelphia, Indiana in Washington County while he was young. His father opened a tannery business, which Winfield worked in while a boy. When the Civil War broke out, Winfield and his brothers enlisted in the 16th Indiana Volunteer Infantry in 1862. The Army rejected him because of an arm injury he had recently suffered. Durban later enlisted in the 139th Regiment Indiana Infantry, which mustered in on June 5, 1864. Durban helped raise a company for the regiment, which went on to the Siege of Vicksburg and duty in Arkansas.

After the War

Durban returned to Indiana after a brief stint attending a small college in St. Louis, Missouri. For a short time, he worked as the bookkeeper for a dry goods store in Indianapolis. After migrating to Anderson, he met and married Bertha McCullough, with whom he would have two children. He worked for his father in law at the Citizens' Bank in Anderson. During this time the Gas Boom occurred. He and his father-in-law founded several small businesses, which allowed him to accumulate a modest amount of wealth. During this time, he became active politically, gaining election to the State Republican Central Committee.

Spanish-American War

The Spanish American War broke out in 1898. Governor James Mount appointed Durbin as colonel in command of the 161st Regiment Indiana Infantry. The recruits of this regiment came mainly from Hammond, Mount Vernon, Shelbyville, Madison, Jeffersonville, Richmond, New Castle,

Rushville, Monticello, Columbus, Michigan City and Lawrenceburg. It mustered in on July 15, 1898. The regiment was part of the Havana occupation during the war. The occupation lasted for three months. The regiment mustered out on April 30, 1899, after which Durbin returned to Indianapolis.

Governor

The Republican Party nominated Durbin for governor in 1900. Durbin won the election, becoming the seventh and last Civil War veteran to serve as Indiana governor. During his term, a major embezzlement scheme at Indiana University surfaced. He threatened to move the university away from Bloomington if university officials did not clear it up. He advocated election reform and set up juvenile courts for young offenders. The growth of the use of automobiles led him to realize the importance of Indiana's central position in the United States. He began advocating for improved roads and highways in the state. He also used firm measures to end the vigilante white cap groups that operated throughout the state. This virtually ended the lawless lynchings that plagued Indiana previously.

Post Governorship

Durbin would run again for governor in 1912, but lose his bid. He remained active in politics and pursued his Anderson business interests. He passed away on December 18, 1928 in Anderson. He is interred in Crown Hill Cemetery in Indianapolis.

Dearborn County Historical Marker - Medal of Honor Citations

Medal of Honor Citations

http://www.hmdb.org/marker.asp?marker=22171

Civil War

By Ginger Drenning, August 23, 2009

Inscription.

Dearborn County

Medal of Honor Citations

Civil War

Name Awarded

Pvt. William Shepherd - - May 3, 1865

Pvt. Frank Stolz - - July 9, 1894

Pvt. David H. Helms - - - July 26, 1894

Pvt. Thomas A. Blasdel - - - August 11, 1894

Pvt. John W. Conaway - - - - August 11, 1894

Pvt. William W. Chisman - - - August 15, 1894

Erected 1966 by Legion Posts of Dearborn County.

Marker series. This marker is included in the Medal of Honor Recipients marker series.

Location. 39° 5.455' N, 84° 50.995' W.

Marker is in Lawrenceburg, Indiana, in Dearborn County.

Marker is on West High Street west of Mary Street, on the right when traveling west.

Located on the left pillar - of the front entry of Dearborn County Courthouse in Lawrenceburg, Indiana.

Marker is at or near this postal address:

215 West High Street, Lawrenceburg IN 47025, United States of America.

Brief History of the Medal of Honor

Established by an act of Congress on December 21, 1861, the law authorized a December 9 resolution introduced by Iowa Senator James W. Grimes. This Medal of Honor was to "promote the efficiency of the Navy," by awarding a medal for acts that went above and beyond the call of duty. Congress authorized an Army version on July 12, 1862. The Air Force received a version on April 14, 1965. The Medal of Honor is awarded only to members of the United States Military. Marines and Coast Guard personnel receive the naval version of the Medal.

Awarding the Medal of Honor

Typically, a request for awarding a Medal of Honor ascends up through the chain of command from the proposed recipient's commanding officer until it reaches the Secretary of Defense, who will pass the recommendation on to a member of Congress. Typically, this member is from the proposed recipients Congressional District. Alternatively, a member of Congress can introduce a resolution without this chain of command. The chain of command process can take up to eighteen months to complete. If Congress approves the resolution to award the Medal of Honor to an individual, the President of the United States personally awards the Medal to the recipient at a White House ceremony, in the name of Congress. If the award is posthumous, or the recipient is unable to participate, the next of kin will receive the award in their stead. Currently Congress has awarded 3,515 Medals of Honor since its establishment during the Civil War.

Current guidelines for awarding the Medal of Honor, established by Congress in 1963:

1. While engaged in an action against an enemy of the United States;

2, while engaged in military operations involving conflict with an opposing foreign force; or,

3, while serving with friendly forces engaged in armed conflict against an opposing armed force in which the United States is not a belligerent party.

Congressional Medal of Honor Society

40 Patriots Point Road

Mt. Pleasant, SC 29464

medalhq@cmohs.org

http://www.cmohs.org/

Historical Marker Project.- Medal of Honor Recipients

http://www.historicalmarkerproject.com/series/87/medal-of-honor-recipients.html

Dearborn County Historical Marker - Vietnam War Memorial

Vietnam War Memorial

http://www.hmdb.org/marker.asp?marker=22202

Dearborn County Indiana

Inscription.

In God We Trust

In Grateful remembrance of the men of Dearborn County who gave their lives in the Vietnam War, erected by the Citizens of Dearborn County, Indiana.

Honor Roll, first column:

William Omer Burkett • Thomas Denning • Larry Arthur Diefenbach • Larry Fogle • Harvey D. Gray • David Hemphill • Donald Ray Henry • Clabe Herald, Jr. • Neil Philip Farmer

Honor Roll, second column:

Ronald A. Hoff • Kenneth Wayne Lozier • Dale K. McLanahan • Ronald W. Montgomery • Richard Wayne Sanders • William M. Treadway • Orville Wells • Robert J. Williamson

Erected by Citizens of Dearborn County.

Location. 39° 5.46' N, 84° 50.988' W.

Marker is in Lawrenceburg, Indiana, in Dearborn County.

Marker is on West High Street west of Mary Street, on the right when traveling west.

Located on the right most front pillar as you face the Dearborn County Courthouse in Lawrenceburg, Indiana.

Marker is at or near this postal address:

215 West High Street, Lawrenceburg IN 47025, United States of America.

By Ginger Drenning, August 23, 2009

2. Long View - - Vietnam War Memorial Marker

Brief History by the Author:

The Vietnam War had its roots in colonial French control of the area then called Indo-China, dating from the 1850's. French colonial rule continued for over seventy years. Various opposition rebel groups fought against French rule, but none had any success. In 1940, the Japanese invaded and occupied the area. The French colonial authorities had allied themselves with the French Vichy regime in France that collaborated with their Nazi conquerors. The Japanese occupiers of Indochina, in turn, collaborated with the French colonial officials. After the Allies drove German troops from France, the Vichy regime collapsed. Fearing the French officials, the Japanese jailed the French and set up a puppet regime in Indo-China. The Japanese troops surrendered to Allied troops in September 1945 after the main Japanese surrender. However, they were the only ones capable of controlling the area, thus the Allies left them in place.

Viet Minh

The Viet Minh had organized in the early 1940's primarily to oppose the French. After the Japanese invasion, they then opposed them. After the Japanese became largely inactive after September 1945, they managed to launch successfully the August Revolution, in which they took command of the country.

British Occupation and Departure

The Allies were adamant that the area still belonged to the French, but as the French had no means to defend or control the country, British forces occupied the southern part of the country and the Nationalist Chinese occupied the north. The Viet Minh won elections across northern Vietnam. They agreed to allow French military personnel to replace the Chinese in exchange for French recognition of the Democratic Republic of Vietnam. French military personnel arrived in Hanoi in March and began a military operation that cleared all the Viet Minh from the city. The British army departed Vietnam in March 1946.

First Indo-China War

The Viet Minh commenced a guerilla war against the French, supported now by the People's Republic of China. The Viet Minh had communist ties and the support of the Communist Chinese reinforced this. The French began receiving United States support in the 1950 in the form of weapons and advisors who helped train the fledgling South Vietnamese Army. The war transitioned from a civil war to a Cold War conflict. At the Battle of Dien Bien Phu Viet Minh forces delivered a devastating defeat to the French. The French subsequently abandoned Viet Nam in 1954. The Viet Minh continued their struggle against the South Vietnamese government, which had gained its independence.

Division of Vietnam

During the 1954 Geneva Conference the Soviet Union, the United States, France, the United Kingdom, and the People's Republic of China came to an agreement that divided Vietnam along the 17th parallel. The United States continued to support the South Vietnam government.

Escalation of the War

President Dwight D. Eisenhower supported the South Vietnamese with weapons and advisors, but resisted expansion of the war. When President Kennedy was inaugurated in 1960, the "Domino Theory" dominated political thought. The fear was that if South Vietnam fell to the communist Viet Minh, the Southeast Asian nations of Laos, Cambodia and Thailand would follow. During the Kennedy administration, United States Military personnel in South Vietnam grew from the 900 advisors placed there by President Eisenhower to 16,000 at the time of Kennedy's assassination. The conflict continued to escalate after

President Lyndon Johnson took office. Fearing a communist takeover after the South Vietnamese regime began to collapse. Johnson increased troop strength during his administration to 265,000 troops.

War Protests

Civil protests against the escalation of the war grew during the middle to late 1960's. Opposition to the war became so politically volatile that President Johnson abandoned his reelection campaign. His Vice President ran and gained the Democratic nomination for President. Richard Nixon gained the Republican nomination and the Presidency in 1968, partly on his proposed " Vietnamization" policy. War protests on college campuses and other places continued, resulting in the Kent Massacre in 1970, in which four college protesters were killed by National Guard troops during a protest.

Drawdown and the Fall of South Vietnam

Nixon began his drawdown of troops in 1970. He escalated it after his 1972 reelection. The last troops left March 5, 1971. Nixon used bombing runs by B-52's to support the South Vietnamese troops. The Democratic Party continued to oppose him, and forced his resignation in 1974 over the Watergate crises. Using the political turmoil created by the resignation, they cut the military support budget to South Vietnam, weakening the regime. The communist insurgents in the south, bolstered by their aid from the Chinese, continued their success against the beleaguered South Vietnamese until Saigon fell on April 30, 1975. United States military helicopters had evacuated the last of the United States officials under heavy gunfire on April 29.

The United States lost 58,315 soldiers and suffered 303,644 wounded during the war.

Dearborn County Historical Markers - The Spirits of Lawrenceburg

The Spirits of Lawrenceburg

By Duane Hall, May 21, 2013

1. The Spirits of Lawrenceburg Marker

Inscription Army Captain Samuel Colville Vance was a surveyor for the United States government living in Cincinnati, Ohio. In 1802, he purchased all the land comprising the original town of "Lawrenceburg." At that time, the land was part of Hamilton County, Ohio. Soon, settlers made their homes near the Ohio River and surrounding creeks. Like many Ohio River towns, Lawrenceburg's economy centered on the Ohio River, and the shipping and related industries it enabled. However, some unusual industries thrived. In the 1800s, cigars were made here, and were considered some of the finest in the world. Lawrenceburg had buggy manufacturers as well. An early automobile, the James Model A Roadster was produced here in 1909.

Distilleries

Distilleries were found in the Lawrenceburg area as early as 1809. By the end of 1855, Lawrenceburg was home to Hobbs Distillery, John H. Gaff & Son, N.J. Walsh Distillery, Nicholas Oester, Frederick Rodenburg & Co. and John B. Garnier Brewery. Purchased in 1933 from the Rossville Distillery Company, the Seagram's plant is a reminder of the distillery days of old Lawrenceburg.

Vance-Tousey House

Visitors can see Captain Vance's spectacular West High Street home that he built in 1818. Known as the Vance-Tousey House, it is considered one of Indiana's finest examples of Federal architecture, and is listed in the National Register of Historic

At the southwest corner of Lawrenceburg Newtown Park

Places. It is now the home of The Dearborn County Historical Society and open to the public.

By the way: Captain Vance named the town Lawrenceburg after his wife's maiden name, Lawrence.

Location. 39° 5.709' N, 84° 51.472' W.

Marker is in Lawrenceburg, Indiana, in Dearborn County.

Marker is at the intersection of 2nd Street and Main Street, on the right when traveling west on 2nd Street.

Marker is located in Lawrenceburg Newtown Park fronting 2nd Street.

Marker is in this post office area: Lawrenceburg IN 47025, United States of America.

Brief History by the Author

Samuel Colville Vance

See Lawrenceburg history

James Model A Roadster

The J. & M. Motor Car Company operated in Lawrenceburg from 1909 until 1911. The company only produced a few of these automobiles during its short lifetime.

Hobbs Distillery

Established during the economic boom that followed the construction of the Whitewater Canal in 1837, a fire destroyed the distillery in 1839. Rebuilt by Hobbs and Craft, fire again ravaged the building in 1850. The distillery ceased operations after the second fire.

John H. Gaff & Son

Businessman John H. Gaff and his brother Thomas built their distillery, the T & J.W. Gaff & Company Distillery, in Lawrenceburg into a nationwide business. For more on the distillery, see Hillforest Mansion. The distillery began operation in 1843 as the T & J.W. Gaff & Company Distillery on the bank of Hogan Creek in Aurora. The distillery merged with the Fleischmann distilleries.

John H. Gaff (September 30, 1820 - February 26, 1879)

The son of James and Margaret Wilson Gaff, Thomas was native to Springfield, New Jersey. After completing his common school education, he apprenticed to a jeweler, Mr. Ackerson in New York City. Tiring of the jeweler's trade, he migrated to Mexico, settling in Mexico City until 1845, when he came to Aurora to join his brother Thomas in the distillery business. During this time in Aurora, he served as mayor for two terms. Sometime in 1851, he moved to Newburgh, New York to marry Margaret G. Lendrum. The couple would have five children. Gaff returned to Aurora in 1864 to continue with the distillery, where he remained until his death in 1879.

Rossville Distillery

Founded in 1847, the Cincinnati based James Walsh & Company acquired it in 1875. The James Walsh & Company operated the distillery in Lawrenceburg until 1932, when a fire destroyed much of the plant. In 1902, the plant has a daily mashing capacity of 5,000 bushels of grain, storage space for 60,000 barrel in its warehouses. Facilities included four steel grain elevators holding 200,000 bushels, and two slop dryers that held 5,000 bushels of feed. The Joseph E Seagram and Sons Company acquired the site in 1933.

Pernod Ricard purchased the plant in 2001 and has continued operations.

John B. Garnier Brewery

Founded by John B. Garnier, the John B. Garnier Brewery operated from 1857 until 1866.

John B. Garnier (August 15 1820 - March 7, 1897)

A native of France, Garnier migrated to the United States in 1845. He came to Lawrenceburg on June 17, 1847, where he opened a malt house. He married Mary E. Dafner, with whom he would have three children. The success of the malt house led to his opening a brewery in 1857. His beer became popular in the Dearborn County area. He would continue brewing beer after the brewery closed until his death in 1897.

Dearborn County Historical Markers - World War II War Memorial

Dearborn County World War II War Memorial

http://www.hmdb.org/marker.asp?marker=22175

World War II War Memorial Marker Photo, Click for full size

By Ginger Drenning, August 23, 2009

1. World War II War Memorial Marker

Inscription.

WORLD WAR II

For God and Country

This tablet is erected in honor of the men who answered their country's call and gave their lives for freedom

Location. 39° 5.457' N, 84° 50.993' W.

Marker is in Lawrenceburg, Indiana, in Dearborn County.

Marker is on West High Street west of Mary Street, on the right when traveling west.

Located on the pillar - to the left of the front door - of the Dearborn County Courthouse in Lawrenceburg, Indiana.

Marker is in this post office area: Lawrenceburg IN 47025, United States of America.

Brief History by the Author

World War II (1939 - 1945)

In Europe

At the end of World War I, most of the European nations blamed Germany for the war and wished to make her pay for it. The Armistice imposed severe reparations on Germany, stripped her of her overseas territories and reduced Germany's home territory. The armistice also imposed restrictions on the size and scope of the German military. The German Empire collapsed in the aftermath, replaced by a republic called the Weimar Republic. The Great Depression combined with severe inflation to produce a horrible economy in Germany. The Nazi leader Adolph Hitler took advantage of the deplorable conditions to maneuver into becoming the Chancellor of Germany in 1933.

Arming for War

Hitler began rearming Germany, defying treaties as he did so. At his direction, Germany signed alliance treaties with Italy and Japan. Hoping to counter the German rise, Great Britain and France signed treaties of alliance. Hitler, in an attempt to prevent the two-war front that had hampered the German military in World War I, signed a non-aggression treaty with the Soviet Union. On September 1, 1939, Germany invaded Poland. Seventeen days later, the Soviet Union invaded Poland from the east. Germany and the Soviet Union divided the nation between them. In 1940 Germany invaded, and conquered, Sweden, Norway, France and several other European countries. By late 1940 Germany, Russia and Italy controlled the European Continent. Britain alone escaped invasion and by late 1940 was engaged in a fight for its life.

War in Asia

Japan had continued its expansionist policy begun in the years before World War I. By 1941, it had invaded China, Indo-China, the Philippines and many other islands and nations in the Pacific Ocean. The Japanese viewed the United States as a threat to its power and its sea-lanes. To knock the United States naval fleet out of the war, the Japanese attacked the naval base on Pearl Harbor in Hawaii on December 7, 1941. The United States declared war on Japan on December 8, 1941. By virtue of the treaties signed by the various nations, Germany and Italy declared war on the United States, who followed suit. By late December 1941, the world was again at war.

A Brief Summary

World War II was a vast conflict involving several theaters, hundreds, if not thousands, of battles. The scale of the war is beyond the scope of this article. After expending vast supplies of lives and treasure, the Allied powers of the United States, Great Britain and France eventually prevailed. Germany had betrayed the Russians and invaded that nation, thus the Soviets joined the alliance against Germany. The Allies invaded continental Europe on June 6, 1944. This invasion, known as D-Day, allowed United States and British forces to establish a tenuous toehold on the continent. It would take almost a year of hard driving warfare to occupy Germany and force surrender on May 8, 1945. The war in the Pacific raged on. The United States employed a strategy called "Island Hopping." They captured Japanese island strongholds one at a time. The names of the battles were many, including Iwo Jima, Guadalcanal, Gwaum and many others. By August 1945, the United States and Britain had captured most of the Japanese fortress islands. Only Japan remained. The Japanese had rejected a demand for unconditional surrender. During the war, the United States had developed a powerful weapon, the atomic bomb. Hoping to force surrender and save thousands of lives, President Harry Truman authorized the use of an atomic bomb. United States bombers delivered two bombs a few days apart, hitting Hiroshima and Nagasaki. The horrible destruction caused by the bombs forced the Japanese to surrender, on August 15, 1945. The cost of the war was dear, over 8 million military deaths and 45 million civilian deaths. United States military deaths totaled 416,800.

Dearborn Historical Marker St. John The Baptist Church Inscription.

Second Oldest Roman Catholic Church in Indiana. Established 1824. Original log meeting house replaced by frame church in 1842. First brick edifice erected 1847. Present church dedicated October 19, 1879.

Erected 1976 by Dearborn County Bicentennial Committee.

Location. 39° 14.67' N, 84° 56.88' W.

Marker is in Dover, Indiana, in Dearborn County.

Marker is on Indiana Route 1 just south of Sawmill Road, on the left when traveling north.

Marker is in this post office area: Guilford IN 47022, United States of America.

Brief History

Established by Irish Catholics, the congregation formed in 1820 at Dover, and then known as McKenzie's Crossroads, the church was built in 1824. It is the second oldest Catholic parish in Indiana, St. Francis Xavier Cathedral and Library in Vincennes being the oldest. many locals still refer to Dover as "Tipperary." The parishioners built a log church in 1824, which they replaced with a wood frame church in 1842. Missionary priests from Cincinnati, Bardstown in Kentucky and Vincennes visited the flock to tend their needs. The parish officially formed in 1840, when permanent church records began. General John Morgan Dearborn County Historical Marker

General John Morgan

1. General John Morgan Marker

Inscription:

Marched east along this road on Monday, July 13, 1863 in his raid across Southern Indiana.

Erected 1927 by Dearborn County Historical Society.

Location. 39° 14.464' N, 84° 56.846' W.

Dover, Indiana, in Dearborn County.

Marker is at the intersection of Indiana Route 1 and North Dearborn Road, on the right when traveling north on State Route 1.

Brief History:

Morgan's Raid (July 8-13, 1863)

Brigadier General John Hunt Morgan, in an effort to draw Union troops away from their campaign in Tennessee, crossed the Ohio River with over 2000 trained and seasoned Confederate troops. Fresh off two raids in Kentucky that rattled Union commanders in the area, he defied orders from his superior General Braxton Bragg, by crossing the Ohio River into Indiana on July 8 and 9, 1863.

John Hunt Morgan (June 1, 1825 – September 4, 1864)

The eldest son of ten children born to Calvin and Henrietta (Hunt) Morgan, John's father migrated to Lexington, Kentucky after the failure of his pharmacy. He attended Transylvania College but the university tossed him out in 1844 for dueling. He enlisted in the Army in 1846 to serve in the Mexican-American War. He had an avid interest in the military and raised a unit in 1852, which the state legislature disbanded. When tensions began rising during the years before the Civil War, he raised another unit in 1857, which he trained well. When war broke out, he did not immediately favor secession. But when the southern states began seceding, he and his men joined the cause. Using his corps of "Lexington Riflemen" as a nucleus, he soon raised a unit, the 2nd Kentucky Cavalry Regiment. This unit fought at the Battle of Shiloh. On July 4, 1862, Morgan launched the first of his Kentucky raids. This successful action resulted in the capture of over a thousand Federal troops and the requisitioning of tons of Union supplies and hundreds of horses. A second series of raids against Union Major General William S. Rosecrans supply lines disrupted the Union troops and created havoc in the Union command in

Kentucky. The success of these raids encouraged his foray into Indiana.

The Crossing

Morgan launched his raid from Burkesville, Kentucky, which is near the Tennessee/Kentucky state line. The beginning of this raid coincided with General Lee's Battle of Gettysburg far to the northeast. From Burkesville, the troops rode north to Brandenburg, Kentucky. He had already scouted the Ohio to find suitable places to cross and had settled on this site. His soldiers commandeered two riverboats on July 7 and by the next day; they moved north towards Corydon and the only Civil War battle to occur on Indiana soil.

Visitors can visit the battlefield here:

Battle of Corydon Memorial Park

100 Old Hwy 135 SW

Corydon, IN 47112

http://www.harrisoncountyparks.com/parks/battle-of-corydon-memorial-park/

After Corydon

Morgan did not rest after his victory at Corydon. He continued east, crossing Harrison, Washington, Scott, Jennings, Jefferson, Ripley and Dearborn counties. Corydon's townspeople cared for Morgan's wounded soldiers from the battle, using the old Presbyterian Church as a hospital.

The Indiana portion of the raid has been mapped into an Auto Tour. The John Hunt Morgan Heritage Trail traces the route of Morgan's Raiders through Indiana as it fled through the countryside into Ohio.

Find out more Morgan's Raiders in Indiana here.

http://www.hhhills.org/John-Hunt-Morgan.html

Dearborn County Historical Markers -A Historic Road Less Traveled

A Historic Road Less Traveled Marker image.

By Duane Hall, May 21, 2013

1. A Historic Road Less Traveled Marker

Inscription.

Who would think that a country road would hold so much history? Old State Highway 56 takes you past the historic Speakman-Tallentire house and to a famous bridge.

Elderly Stephen S. Speakman was in love with a young Kentucky belle who agreed to marry him if he built her a magnificent house. With the help of slave labor borrowed from his bride's Kentucky home, the elegant Greek Revival-style Speakman-Tallentire house was completed in 1845. It sits on a rise near the Laughery Creek. Although now overgrown, it once had a view of the Creek, and across the Ohio River to Kentucky. Bricks used to build it were made right on the premises. The home is now a private residence, not open to the public, and should be viewed from the roadside.

Travel past the Speakman-Tallentire House and see the three-span, 302 foot "Triple Whipple Bridge," built in 1878 that joins Ohio and Dearborn Counties. It is the only remaining bridge of its type in the country, and is named for the nineteenth century bridge designer Squire Whipple, who designed a special system of supports. The bridge's historic significance earned it a place in the National Register

A Historic Road Less Traveled Marker image. Click for full size.

By Duane Hall, May 21, 2013

2. A Historic Road Less Traveled Marker

Old State Road 56 is behind the marker

of Historic Places. The bridge is presently closed to vehicular traffic but has been rehabilitated for pedestrian use.

Visitors are encouraged to visit a neighboring Ohio River Scenic site just to the north of here at Riverview Cemetery.

By the Way: Indiana has more than 6,000 bridges, many of them considered historic treasures.

Topics.

This historical marker is listed in these topic lists: Bridges & Viaducts Notable Buildings.

Location.

39° 1.267' N, 84° 53.02' W. Marker is near Aurora, Indiana, in Ohio County. Marker is at the intersection of Hartford Pike and Old State Road 56, on the right when traveling north on Hartford Pike. Touch for map. Marker is in this post office area: Aurora IN 47001, United States of America.

https://www.hmdb.org/m.asp?m=66899

https://www.hmdb.org/m.asp?m=100075

Exhausted Morgan Troops

Inscription.

Located on the southeast corner of State Road 101 and County Road 900N stands the Ferris Schoolhouse. The structure still stands and has been converted to a private residence. General Morgan spent the evening of July 12, 1863, inside the school while his exhausted troopers camped at the present-day St. Paul cemetery. Morgan and his

Raiders had ridden approximately 45 miles that day (150 miles in the last four days).

Two miles to the north at Sunman, 1,800 Union soldiers were waiting in railroad cars for orders to pursue Morgan and his men. At 5 a.m. on the 13th, Morgan and his men continued their raid eastward (on Asche Road or County Road 900N) into Dearborn County.

Erected by Historic Hoosier Hills RC&D. (Marker Number 20.)

Topics and series. This historical marker is listed in this topic list: War, US Civil. In addition, it is included in the John Hunt Morgan Heritage Trail in Indiana series list.

Location. 39° 12.296' N, 85° 5.664' W. Marker is in Sunman, Indiana, in Ripley County a short distance from the Dearborn County line.

Exhausted Morgan Troops Marker image. Click for full size.

By Tom Bosse, October 14, 2016

2. Exhausted Morgan Troops Marker

is on State Road 101 north of Asche Road, on the right when traveling north. Marker is located near the entrance to the St. Paul Cemetery. Touch for map. Marker is at or near this postal address: 8930 State Rte 101, Sunman IN 47041, United States of America.

Dillsboro Historical Marker

Inscription

The town was laid out by Mathias Whetstone in 1830, and named for General James Dill, soldier in the War of 1812, first county recorder, a member of the Indiana 1816 Constitutional Convention, military associate and friend of

Generals William Henry Harrison, Arthur St. Clair and Captain Samuel C. Vance.

Dillsboro Historical Marker

Erected 1976 by Dearborn County Bicentennial Committee.

Location. 39° 1.162' N, 85° 3.662' W.

Marker is at the intersection of Front Street and Bank Street, on the left when traveling north on Front Street.

Located at the Town Office and Fire Station.

For more on Dillsboro's history, see the Dillsboro entry.

Dearborn Historical Marker - Abraham Lincoln

Indiana (Dearborn County), Lawrenceburg — Abraham Lincoln

Inscription.

Abraham Lincoln made a famous pre-inaugural speech from his train platform near here Feb. 12, 1861, placing emphasis on the people's part in justice and good government.

Erected 1966 by Dearborn County Sesquicentennial Committee.

Marker series.

This marker is included in the Lincoln 1861 Inaugural Train Stops marker series.

Location.

39° 5.517' N, 84° 50.778' W.

Marker is in Lawrenceburg, Indiana, in Dearborn County.

Marker can be reached from South Walnut Street south of New Street.

Marker is at the Ohio River at the South end of Walnut Street.

Marker is in this post office area: Lawrenceburg IN 47025, United States of America.

Brief History

The marker denotes the spot that Abraham Lincoln stopped for a speech during his inaugural tour that began on February 11, 1861. He would stop at ten cities in Indiana before entering Ohio.

Abraham Lincoln

Abraham Lincoln spent his boyhood years in southern Indiana. Lincoln State Park preserves some of the sites and memories important to Lincoln as he was growing up. Nancy Hanks Lincoln presented her husband Thomas with a son on February 12, 1809. He was born on the Sinking Spring Farm in Hardin County, Kentucky. When Abraham was a boy of seven, Thomas moved the family to southern Indiana. Thomas had been a wealthy Kentucky farmer until 1816, when he lost all his land due to faulty property line disputes. He moved his family to Indiana where the property laws provided better title to land. Thomas was also staunchly anti-slavery. Kentucky was a slave state while Indiana was not.

Abraham would live in Spencer County in Indiana until March, 1830 when the Lincoln family moved to Decatur, Illinois. During their stay in Indiana, Abe's mother, Nancy Hanks Lincoln would die of "milk sickness," and his sister Sarah would die during childbirth. Lincoln obtained his law degree in Illinois and began his political career there, culminating with his successful run for President in 1860. Lincoln began his Whistle stop tour on Monday, February 11, 1861 at Springfield, Illinois.

131

Whistle Stop Tour

Springfield Train Station

As Lincoln boards the train at Springfield's Great Western Railroad depot, he says to the crowd, "To this place, and the kindness of these people, I owe everything... I now leave.. with a task before me greater than that which rested upon [George] Washington."

Decatur Train Depot

Tolono Train Station

Vermilion Country Train Depot

State Line City, Indiana

After being joined by a committee of Indiana politicians in State Line City, Lincoln speaks before a crowd in Lafayette, "While some of us may differ in political opinions, still we are all united in one feeling for the Union. We all believe in the maintenance of the Union, of every star and every stripe of the glorious flag, and permit me to express the sentiment that upon the union of the States, there shall be between us no difference. "

Lafayette, Indiana

Thorntown, Indiana

Lebanon, Indiana

Zionsville, Indiana

Indianapolis, Indiana

Thorntown, Indiana

Lebanon, Indiana

Zionsville, Indiana

Indianapolis, Indiana

Lincoln arrives at 5 p.m., welcomed by Gov. Oliver Morton and a 34-gun salute. He joins a procession of 20,000 state legislators, public employees, soldiers, firemen and others. For the first time in his journey, he temporarily loses his copies of his Inaugural address.

With Mrs. Lincoln alongside him, he boards the train en route to Cincinnati at 11 a.m. the following morning.

Tuesday, February 12, 1861

Shelbyville, Indiana

Greensburg, Indiana

Morris, Indiana

Lawrenceburg, Indiana

Cincinnati, Ohio

At a public reception held by the German Industrial Association, Lincoln says, "I deem it my duty...that I should wait until the last moment, for a development of the present national difficulties before I express myself decidedly what course I shall pursue."

His reluctance to make definitive public statements on the secession crisis was an ongoing theme in his remarks on this journey.

Escorted by members of the Ohio legislature, Lincoln departed on the Little Miami Railroad at 9 a.m. the following morning.

For more information about Lincoln's Whistle Stop Tour, contact:

http://www.smithsonianmag.com/history/lincolns-whistle-stop-trip-to-washington-161974/

Indiana Historical Bureau Markers

Title of Marker:

Canal Junction

Location:

NW corner of Whitewater River bridge at Campbell & State Streets across railroad tracks, south side of West Harrison. (Dearborn County, Indiana)

Installed by:

1999 Indiana Historical Bureau, Canal Society of Indiana, and Dearborn County Historical Society.

Marker ID #:

15.1999.1

Marker Text:

Side one:

The Whitewater Canal and the Cincinnati and Whitewater Canal joined in Harrison to provide better access to Cincinnati markets and Ohio River. Indiana Internal Improvement Act 1836 authorized Whitewater Canal; completed from Brookville to Lawrenceburg 1839. Nearby Dam No. 1 on Whitewater River created a pool for canal boats to cross the river.

Side two:

Cincinnati and Whitewater Canal incorporated by Ohio General Assembly 1837. Completed seven miles from Harrison (now West Harrison), Indiana to Dry Fork Creek, Ohio 1840. Twenty-five mile canal opened 1843 when 1, 782 foot tunnel completed at Cleves, Ohio. Traffic diverted to Cincinnati on this interstate transportation link diminished Lawrenceburg's importance as a market.

Brief History by the Author

Canals reigned supreme during the early part of the Nineteenth Century before the advent of the railroads. They provided a cheap, fast means of transporting goods overland. They had grave disadvantages, though. They were expensive to build and maintain. It was only possible to construct them in favorable terrain. Indiana and Ohio both embarked on canal building programs and managed to link their systems here, at the junction of the Cincinnati and Whitewater Canal and the Whitewater Canal.

Whitewater Canal

The Whitewater Canal's construction lasted from 1836 to 1847. During this time, there were many starts and pauses as the State of Indiana ran out of money and the various private companies charged with completing also ran into financial difficulties. After completion, it connected Hagerstown, Indiana with Cincinnati, Ohio seventy-six miles to the south. The canal provided a quick, convenient way for farmers to transport their goods to market in the cities. Before the canal a farmer would need several days travel over deeply rutted roads to take his goods to Cincinnati. The canal proved a difficult construction project. It dropped 491 feet over the distance and needed fifty-six locks and seven dams. Several aqueducts to carry the canal over waterways also needed construction. The canal operated until 1862. The Whitewater Valley Railroad runs a part of the canal as a tourist attraction between Connersville and Metamora Indiana. The train runs alongside the canal and at Metamora visitors can ride a canal boat. The town of Metamora has many small shops and museums. The State of Indiana maintains an operating gristmill in the town.

For more information contact:

Whitewater Valley Railroad

455 Market St,

Connersville, IN 47331

(765) 825-2054

http://www.whitewatervalleyrr.org/main.php

Cincinnati and Whitewater Canal

When Indiana proposed building the Whitewater Canal, Cincinnati merchants persuaded a consortium of private investors and the State of Ohio to fund a spur to connect with it. This fourteen miles spur was constructed between 1839 and 1843. It included a canal tunnel, one of the few constructed in the United States. The canal was eventually abandoned and has silted up over the years from flooding and disuse. The Indianapolis and Cincinnati Railroad purchased the canal in 1862 and used the canal towpath for a rail line. The tunnel, used for a time as a railroad tunnel, still exists and is on the National Register of Historic Places. President William Henry Harrison owned part of the land the canal needed and donated some land towards it. He is buried on a ridge over the tunnel. The Ohio Title of Marker:

Greenville Treaty Line

Location:

Location: SR 101 and SR 48, south of Sunman near Negangards Corner

Installed by:

Erected by the Indiana Historical Bureau, 1966

Marker ID #:

15.1966.2 and 15.1966.3

Marker Text:

The western boundary of Dearborn and Ohio Counties follows the old Indian boundary line established by General Anthony Wayne with northwestern Indians at Greenville, Ohio, August 3, 1795.

Note: this marker no longer stands. The author included it because the Greenville Treaty line forms the boundary between Ripley and Dearborn Counties.

General Anthony Wayne defeated a consortium of Amerindian tribes at the Battle of Fallen Timbers. The Greenville Treaty signed a year later established new boundaries between the Amerindian tribes and the encroaching whites.

Battle of Fallen Timbers

The native tribes had signed a treaty with the British in 1768 called the Treaty of Fort Stanwix. In this treaty the British designated certain lands north of the Ohio as belonging to the native tribes. At the conclusion of the Revolution, the Americans no longer honored the Treaty of Fort Stanwix. They cited a clause in the Treaty of Paris in which the British ceded lands owned by the tribes. The tribes asserted that the British could not give away lands that did not belong to them and that they did not sign that treaty. Encroachment by whites into their territories continued and the natives responded by attacking them. General Anthony Wayne formed an army of 2000 soldiers that he called the Legion of the United States, He marched out of Fort Washington, near Cincinnati, and traveled north. He built a string of forts along the way. The natives watched and waited. They formed a defensive line in an area where a storm had blown all the trees down (fallen timbers) and waited for Wayne. The battle began on August 20 1794 and did not last long. Wayne dealt the native force a decisive defeat.

Greenville Treaty

The consortium of tribes, known as the Western Confederacy, signed the Greenville Treaty at Fort Greenville on August 3, 1795. General Anthony Wayne represented the United States Government and signed the treaty. The signing ended hostilities for a time and established a new boundary between the whites and the natives. The line extended south from the mouth of the Cuyahoga River as it emptied into Lake Erie. It followed the River south to a portage point between it and the Tuscarawas River. From that point it followed the Tuscarawas to Fort Laurens. At Fort Laurens it ran southwest to Fort Loramie on the Great Miami River. From Fort Loramie it ran northwest to Fort Recovery, near the headwaters of the Wabash River and the boundary of current states of Ohio and Indiana. From Fort Recovery it ran to the Ohio River to a point on the north bank of the river across from Carrolton, Kentucky. It is this portion of the Greenville Treaty line that forms the current boundary of Dearborn and Ohio Counties in Indiana. Historical Society has a historical marker near its northern portal.

Title of Marker:

Kibbey's Road

Location:

Location: SR 350 on border of Dearborn and Ripley Co. (Dearborn / Ripley County, Indiana)

Installed by:

Erected by Indiana Sesquicentennial Commission, 1966

Marker ID #:

15.1966.1, 69.1966.1

Marker Text:

The first road to cross Indiana was blazed by Captain Ephraim Kibbey in 1799-1800. This two-hundred mile route ran from Cincinnati to Vincennes, crossing the Greene Ville Treaty Line here.

Note: this marker no longer stands. The author included it because the road was a key entry point for many settlers streaming into the area.

Major Ephraim Kibbey carved the first road to cross what would become the State of Indiana. The two year task began in 1799 and finished in 1800.

Major Ephraim Kibbey (1754 - 1809)

New Jersey native Ephraim Kibbey joined the army during the American Revolution at the beginning of the conflict and served until it ended. A trained land surveyor, he traveled west to the mouth of the Little Miami River on the Ohio River in 1788 and became one of the first settlers of Columbia, Ohio. He joined the team of surveyors that worked at surveying the Symmes Purchase, exposed to harsh conditions and attacks by the natives. He joined the forces of General Anthony Wayne in his efforts to subdue the Amerindian tribes of the area. He served as Captain of the rangers that scouted the vast forests, keeping track of the warriors movements for the General. After the Battle of Fallen Timbers in 1794, peace returned to the Ohio River Valley area and Kibbey returned to his surveying work.

Kibbey's Road

In 1799 he began cutting a road through the forests that would lead from the Great Miami River to Vincennes on the Wabash River. After surveying and cutting about seventy miles of road, Kibbey and his crew became separated. he hunted for his companions unsuccessfully and returned to

Columbia starved and thin. he had subsisted on roots for several days while traveling through the forest. he returned to surveying the road and completed it sometime in 1800. he reported the road as being somewhat over 155 miles in length. The route of this road is known in several places. It went through present day French Lick and portions of it survive in the Hoosier National Forest. A one-half mile section of old trail in Martin County is part of this old road. It met the Buffalo Trace, following that ancient route to Vincennes.

Title of Marker

Lochry's Defeat

Location:

On SR 56 near the Ohio County-Dearborn County line, at the southeast corner of the bridge crossing Laughery Creek. (Ohio County, Indiana)

Erected by:

The Sons of the American Revolution, 1961

ID# : 58.1961.1

Text

On Aug. 24, 1781, Col. Archibald Lochry and 107 recruits for Gen. Clark were ambushed at Lochry Creek by Joseph Brant's raiders. One-third were killed, the rest captured. Lochry and the wounded were later murdered.

Brief History by the Author:

Archibald Lochry (April 15, 1733 — August 24, 1781)

The son of Jeremiah Loughery and Mary Murphy, Archibald was native to Octorarro Settlement, Ireland. The family migrated to York County, Pennsylvania sometime in the late 1730's. At maturity, Archibald became a powerful man, acquiring land and holding several political posts. He gained his first military experience during the latter stages of the French and Indian War when he enlisted on July 18, 1763.

Revolutionary War

In 1781, Lochry received an appointment to serve as colonel in the militia and given authority to recruit 200 men to launch attacks against the native tribes that were attacking the Pennsylvania frontier as part of the hostilities of the Revolutionary War. Since many were reluctant to leave their homes defenseless during a time of conflict, Lochry was only able to recruit 107 men. The company was ready to move by July 1781. Lochry had agreed to join an expedition led by General George Rogers Clark of Virginia on an expedition that was to move down the Ohio River and recruit men in Kentucky. From there they would either move against Fort Detroit or attack Delaware and Shawnee tribes deep in the heart of Indian country in current Indiana and Ohio. These tribes were harassing the Pennsylvania frontier.

The Campaign

Clark departed down the Ohio first from Wheeling. Initially, the two groups were to leave Wheeling together. However, Clark had a serious problem with desertion. Reluctant to leave their homes for extended periods leaving their families undefended, the soldiers deserted in large numbers. This drove Clark to try to move further west faster than anticipated in the hopes of cutting down on desertions. Lochry arrived at Wheeling on August 8, only to find that Clark had already left. Lochry's men built boats and departed Wheeling after spending a few days building them. While there, Lochry sent a canoe downstream with a message to Clark relating that they were low on supplies for both men, horses, and would follow Clark as soon as they could. This message did not reach General Clark. Forces led by George Girty and Chief Joseph Brandt intercepted the messages and began immediately to assemble a force to attack Lochry.

Lochry's Massacre

After departing Wheeling, Lochry kept his boats to the middle of the Ohio River to prevent attack from the shore. Girty and Brandt shadowed the force onshore as it made its way downriver. After several days of travel, Lochry had to go ashore to allow the horses to graze and obtain food for his men. They landed near the mouth of present day Laughery Creek. They killed a buffalo and prepared to cook it while the horses grazed. Meanwhile, danger gathered in the woodland surrounding them. The numbers Brandt and Girty had to attack are not certain, somewhere between 150 and 500 warriors attacked Lochry's force, catching them by surprise. In the short battle that followed, the natives forced Lochry to surrender. About thirty-seven died in the attack, including Lochry, who was reportedly tomahawked as he sat on a log after the surrender. The remainder of the prisoners were marched up trails by the Miami River. The natives ransomed some, killed some and adopted others. Only around twenty-five survived the attack.

Clark's proposed attack against Detroit died with Lochry's Massacre. Lacking the manpower to carry it out, he abandoned the plan. His capture of Vincennes in 1779 would not be repeated at Detroit.

A government clerk on the first documents misspelled the name 'Laughery', and the name has remained unchanged. Riverview Cemetery, the approximate location of the battle near Aurora, contains a monument to Lochry and his men, and a list of the soldiers who took part in the battle in addition to his marker.

Dearborn County Underground Railroad

Residents of Dearborn County, Indiana became active in the Underground Railroad quite early. The East Fork Methodist Protestant Church in the Guilford area formed an antislavery group as early as 1834. There were many county residents involved in aiding escaped slaves on their road north to freedom. Many of the slaves during the 1850 - 1854 period were helped by a former slave blacksmith named Elijah Anderson who claimed to have helped over 1000 slaves escape. From Aurora and Lawrenceburg many of the slaves were spirited along the route now occupied by Indiana State Road 350 to Old Milan. The Old Milan Road, which was formerly called the Aurora Road, took the escaping slaves to points in Ripley County.

Other slaves were taken by night along the railroad tracks because the trains did not run at night. The current CSX railroad from Lawrenceburg to Osgood, Indiana was used for this.

The Underground Railroad

Escaping slaves had several routes from which to choose, depending upon the region they originated. The largest percentage of refugee slaves passing through Southeastern Indiana would have escaped bondage in Tennessee or Kentucky. Others filtered up from the Deep South states of Alabama, Mississippi, or Louisiana. The route escaping slaves took when fleeing bondage was never a static route, it changed constantly due to many factors.

Escaping Slavery

Many groups took on the challenge of helping slaves escape bondage. Forefront in this movement were groups like the American Colonization Society and the Quakers. Many of these groups used agents to go south of the Ohio River to aid slaves wishing to flee. Free blacks often volunteered to perform this service. If caught, they faced imprisonment for the crime of, "enticing a slave."

Slaves escaping bondage from the south faced many obstacles. Most slave owners kept the slaves illiterate, so they could not read or write. Thus, newspapers, maps and other written media were useless to them. Their knowledge of the surrounding countryside was limited, thus once they were out of their immediate area, they could not know who to trust. Slaves along the Ohio River often used it as an avenue of escape. Before the United States Corps of Engineers built the dam and lock system along the river, water levels were much lower. In winter, the river commonly froze over. Slaves living in northern Kentucky often walked across the ice to Indiana. There are some tales of escaping slaves rowing boats across the river. Legend holds that slave holders in northern Kentucky moved their slaves south in winter to get them away from the river.

Across the River

Free blacks mostly lived in separate communities in Indiana, as well as other free states. There were communities of free blacks in Madison, Evansville and other river towns. Frequently, escaping slaves sought out these communities, as they would blend in better there than in a white community. Many free blacks were willing to help them. From this haven, they could plan their move away from the United States and into Canada.

Underground Railroad Terminology

Various people in this clandestine network acquired names that belied their role. People that guided the refugees along the way and provided them with refuge, at great personal risk, were called "Conductors." The homes and businesses used to harbor the refugees became known as "Stations." The conductors referred to the refugees as "Passengers." Frequently, free blacks traveled into the south, a dangerous enterprise, to find those that wished to escape and guided them north. These free blacks were called "Pilots." "Bounty Hunters," sought out the escapees on their journey north to capture them and return them to their owners. The conductors did not keep records of their activities, as these would be incriminating and if authorities found them they could use them to convict the conductors and send them to prison. For this reason, finding information about the participants in the Underground Railroad can be difficult to find.

Fugitive Slave Act of 1850

This act reinforced the Fugitive Slave Act of 1793. This act made aiding and abetting an escaping slave a crime and placed fines on those that defied it. Slave hunters, or bounty hunters, had only posters and flyers to use in their search. The Fugitive Slave Act of 1850 reinforced this act with stricter fines and penalties. The Fugitive Slave Act of 1850 slapped severe penalties on those that aided slaves in their escape. The Act authorized Federal Marshals to capture blacks and it allowed local law enforcement in free states to assist them. Private citizens were also allowed to capture escaping slaves for the reward. These people became known as bounty hunters. A bounty hunter, with only an obscure affidavit, could capture escaping blacks and return them to their owner. Bounty hunters roamed the free northern states searching for escaping blacks and presented an additional peril to the refugees. Congress repealed this law in 1864 during the ravages of the Civil War.

The Underground Railroad Network

This network expanded after the passage of the Fugitive Slave Act. Many northerners felt that the Federal Government had overstepped its boundaries by interfering with their opposition to slavery. Many historians estimate that over 100,000 slaves escaped bondage using this obscure network that snaked northward from the Ohio River to Canada. This network changed constantly, as conductors many times either died, or sold their homes, which necessitated a change. These changes could occur quickly, so a working knowledge of active conductors was necessary. The route could change due to bounty hunter activity, unavailability of a conductor, or other reasons. Movement occurs mostly at night and at random patterns. An escapee might move north, then east, then west and finally north again, depending upon many different circumstances. Eventually, if all went well, the escaping slaves reached Canada, which provided a safe haven.

Three Main Categories

The anti-slavery movement consisted of three general categories of people opposed to slavery. The Free Soil movement, embodied in the Free Soil political party, hoped to restrict slavery to the areas it was already legal and prevent its spread into new territories. Middle of the road anti-slavery advocates wanted to outlaw slavery gradually, over a long period. Abolitionists believed that the practice of slavery was a sin and called for an immediate end to the practice. The abolitionists were willing to go to great lengths, sometimes breaking the law and risking imprisonment, to spirit escaping slaves away to freedom using the complex Underground Railroad system. Most members of this network did not document much of their work, as it was illegal. Thus, finding historical evidence of an individual's involvement can be tricky or even impossible.

Free Soil Party

Founded in 1848 as an anti-slavery party, the Free Soil existed from 1848 through 1854, when the new Republican Party absorbed it. The party comprised anti-slavery Whigs and Democrats. The party was strongest in New York, but existed in several others. The Free Soil Party opposed extending slavery into the territories. The party nominated candidates for President and Vice-President two different times. In 1848, the party nominated Martin Van Buren as President and Charles Francis Adams as Vice President. The ticket garnered no electoral votes, polling at around 10%. In 1852, the party nominated John P. Hale as President and George Washington Julian as Vice President. The ticket this time dropped to less than 5% of the vote. The party did elect two Senators and sixteen representatives to Congress before fading away in 1854 with the rise of the anti-slavery Republican Party.

Underground Railroad in Indiana

The Underground Railroad was a vast network of people in the North and South who aided fugitive slaves in their flight from slavery. In Indiana the route stretched from communities on the Ohio River to the Michigan border. From Michigan the fugitives fled to Canada and freedom. Forefront in this movement was groups like the American Colonization Society and the Quakers. Many of these groups used agents to go south of the Ohio River to aid slaves wishing to flee.

For more information about the Underground Railroad in Indiana, visit this Indiana Historical Bureau link.

http://www.in.gov/history/3119.htm

Dearborn County Cemeteries

Author Note:

It is beyond the scope of this book to delve into all of the cemeteries in Dearborn County. Below is the cemetery listing. For more information, consult these links

https://www.findagrave.com/cemetery-browse/USA/Indiana/Dearborn-County?id=county_806

http://sites.rootsweb.com/~indearbo/Pages/cem.shtml

https://ldsgenealogy.com/IN/Dearborn-County-Cemetery-Records.htm

Alden Cemetery

Cemetery

Aurora

Beatty Cemetery

Cemetery

Bonnell

Braysville

Bright

Cambridge Cemetery

Cemetery

Carbaugh Cemetery

Cemetery

Cheek Cemetery

Cemetery

Cold Springs

Concord Cemetery

Cemetery

Dillsboro

Dover

Ebenezer Baptist Church Cemetery

Cemetery

Eden Cemetery

Cemetery

Farmers Retreat

Ferris Family Cemetery

Cemetery

Five Points Cemetery

Cemetery

Georgetown Cemetery

Cemetery

Greendale

Guard Cemetery

Cemetery

Guilford

Heaton Cemetery

Cemetery

Hogan Hill Cemetery

Cemetery

Hubbells Corner

Huber-Briggs Cemetery

Cemetery

Kyle Family Cemetery

Cemetery

Lawrenceburg

Lawrenceville

Lindsay Family Cemetery

Cemetery

Logan

Logan Cemetery

Cemetery

Lowes Cemetery

Cemetery

Manchester

Manchester Cemetery

Cemetery

Manchester Township

Moores Hill

Mount Sinai

New Alsace

Olcott Cemetery

Cemetery

Rand Cemetery

Cemetery

Record Cemetery

Cemetery

Saint Jacobs Cemetery

Cemetery

Saint Leon

Saint Pauls Catholic Cemetery

Cemetery

Sparta

Sparta Township

Transier Cemetery

Cemetery

Trester Cemetery

Cemetery

Turner Cemetery

Cemetery

Washington Township

Weisburg

West Fork Cemetery

Cemetery

West Harrison

Whiteford Cemetery

Cemetery

Wilmington

Windsor Cemetery

Cemetery

Wrights Corner

Yorkville

Dearborn County Parks

Aurora City Parks

Aurora City Park

Aurora Pool

Aurora Dog Park

Ron Nocks Memorial Park

Largent Field

Aurora Sports Complex

Dearborn Trail

Lesko Park

Mary Stratton Park

Waterways Park

Aurora City Parks

City of Aurora

PO Box 158

Aurora, Indiana 47001

812-926-1777

https://aurora.in.us/parks.html

Bright Parks

Bright Meadows Park

The Sunman-Dearborn School Board donated the initial acreage for Bright Meadows Park in 1996. The Parks Board acquired more land in 2010 to bring it up to the current 18.6 acres.

Bright Meadows Park has two baseball fields, a soccer/pee-wee football field, half-court basketball facility, fitness path, playground, shelter houses and two parking areas. The park also includes several paved walking trails.

Bright Meadows Park

2095 Einsel Road

Bright

http://www.dearborncountyin.us/Parks/bright_meadows_community_park.html

Dillsboro Parks

Dillsboro Community Park

Amenities include: 4 baseball/softball fields, 3 soccer fields, playground equipment, walking trail, and 3 shelters that can be reserved.

Access from Indiana State Road 62. Front Street turns into Arlington Road just outside of town.

A form to reserve the shelters can be found at

http://www.townofdillsboro.com/department/index.php?structureid=19

Dillsboro Community Park

9495 Front St

Dillsboro, IN 47018

https://www.facebook.com/pages/Dillsboro-Community-Park/112298562158784

Heritage Point Park

Bank and North Streets

Dillsboro, IN

This park, at the center of Dillsboro, contains the veteran's memorial, a clock and some landscaping.

Greendale Parks

Lorey Park

Schnebelt Park

Danny Miller Park

Greendale City Park

Cook Park

Homestead Park

Greendale

500 Ridge Avenue

Greendale, IN 47025

812-537-9219

http://www.cityofgreendale.net/parks

Guilford

Guilford Covered Bridge Park

Indiana State Road 1 and York Ridge Road

Guilford, Indiana

Guilford Covered Bridge Park is the site of the recently restored Guilford Covered Bridge, a major county landmark and frequent roadside tourist attraction, as well as an excellent family a gathering area with access to Tanners Creek.

Cars are permitted to drive through the wrought iron gates, across the Guilford Covered Bridge and park in the lower lot. A small shelter house, basketball court, play equipment and bathroom are located in the central open space.

4785 Main St, Guilford, IN 47022

Guilford, Indiana 47022

For more information on the bridge, see the listing for Guilford.

Lawrenceburg Indiana Parks

Cook Park

George Street Park

Ice Skating Rink

Lawrenceburg Babe Ruth Baseball Field

Lawrenceburg Skate Park

Ludlow Hill Park

Newtown Park

Oakey Park

Pat O'Neill Memorial Pool

Ratliff Landing

Todd Creech Park

Arch Street Park

Lawrenceburg Indiana Parks

105B Walnut Street

Lawrenceburg, IN 47025

https://www.thinklawrenceburg.com/category/attractions/parks-featured/

http://www.traillink.com/trail/dearborn-trails-(aurora---lawrenceburg---greendale).aspx

http://www.indianatrails.com/content/dearborn-county-trail-aurora-lawrenceburg-greendale

http://www.traillink.com/trail/dearborn-trails-(aurora---lawrenceburg---greendale).aspx

Dearborn County Parks

Gladys Russel Wildlife Refuge

Dearborn Trails – Aurora – Lawrenceburg – Greendale Indiana

Harry H. And Alma Rullman Wildlife Refuge

County Farm Park

Dearborn County Park & Recreation Board

229 Main Street, Aurora, In 47001

812-926-1189

https://www.dearborncountyparks.com/

Dearborn County Nature Preserves

Buttonwood

Oxbow Properties

Hilltop Farm

Dearborn Trails – Aurora – Lawrenceburg – Greendale Indiana

Winner of the Mid America Trails and Greenway Award in 2007, Dearborn Trail spans three river cities waterfronts on the Ohio River. The trail is about 4.5 miles in total length one-way. Most of the trail is paved and is open year round. The trail connects Greendale, Lawrenceburg and Aurora, Indiana. It begins at the intersection of East William and High Street in Greendale. Dearborn Trail ends in Lesko Park in Aurora, Indiana near Indiana State Road 56. For much of its length it overlooks the Ohio River. The trail uses a restored railroad bridge to cross Tanner's Creek. Hikers and bikers will find benches at various points along the trail. Lesko Park has restrooms, picnic areas and benches. Downtown areas of Greendale, Lawrenceburg and Aurora are a short walk from the trail. An active rail line, the CSX, parallels the trail. The section between Aurora and Lawrenceburg is wooded. Hikers and bikers may see deer, beaver, foxes, waterfowl and shorebirds in this rich wetland area.

Tanners Creek Bridge

https://bridgehunter.com/in/dearborn/tanners-creek/

The Cincinnati and Southern Ohio River Railway constructed the bridge in 1872. Athens Pennsylvania bridge builder Kellogg & Maurice Bridge Company designed and constructed the bridge. Railroads that have used the bridge include:

Big Four

Cleveland, Cincinnati, Chicago & St. Louis Railway (CCC&StL)

New York Central Railroad (NYC)

Penn Central Railroad (PC)

Approximate latitude, longitude

+39.07982, -84.87082 (decimal degrees)

39°04'47" N, 84°52'15" W (degrees°minutes'seconds")

Approximate UTM coordinates

16/684170/4327792 (zone/easting/northing)

Bridgehunter.com ID - BH 42555

Oxbow

The Oxbow is a broad floodplain where the Great Miami River empties into the Ohio. This area where three states - Ohio, Indiana, and Kentucky - come together, is near Lawrenceburg, Indiana, seventeen miles downstream from Cincinnati.

The Oxbow is a heavily-used staging area where migrating birds refuel and rebuild their energies. The area is essential to their success on long flights between distant northern breeding grounds and southern wintering areas. Without the Oxbow these migrants might reach their northern nesting areas without the reserve strength essential to raising new broods of healthy young birds.

To get to the upper Oxbow parking area go south on US Hwy 50 from the I-275 #16 exit. In about 200 yards, turn left (east) at the edge of the Shell/Subway and go over the levee to the front of the cement plant. Turn right and go to the Oxbow entrance sign. Turn left into the Oxbow. The upper parking area is immediately on the right .

Oxbow, Inc

P. O. Box 4172

Lawrenceburg, IN 47025

513-948-8630

http://oxbowinc.org/index.html

Buttonwood Nature Preserve

Buttonwood

10146 South Hogan Road

Moore's Hill, Indiana 47032

http://oakheritageconservancy.org/2015/09/09/buttonwood/

Hilltop Farm

28538 Dunevant Drive

West Harrison, IN 47060

http://oakheritageconservancy.org/2015/09/09/hilltop-

Dearborn County Fair

The Dearborn County Agricultural Society, formed on April 10, 1852 with Seth Platt as president. The association held the first Dearborn County Fair in Manchester on October 27, 28, 29, 1852. . Expenses $113.00, receipts 261.75. this fair was successful, encouraging the sponsors to raise ticket prices. The fair remained in Manchester until 1856 when the Society leased nine acres of land shaded by a grove of sugar maple trees in Aurora. this property is now the Aurora City Park. The circular drive was originally a race track. Two years later a rivalry between Aurora and Lawrenceburg arose over which should host the county fair. The first classes began and included sheep, cattle, hogs, poultry. the Home Economics portion included instructions on jelly making, fruit butters, pickles, baking, needlework Both cities held fairs in 1858, a situation that would continue until 1869, when the Lawrenceburg Agriculture Association formed and the fair moved to Lawrenceburg.

Lawrenceburg Agricultural Association

Lawrenceburg Agricultural Association formed in 1879 and held their first fair on the old fairgrounds in 1880 at the end of center street. They later purchased 8 acres which allowed them to construct a 1/2 mile race track, which gained the reputation as the finest in the country. The grandstand held 2500 people It rained every day during this fair, however attendance was still good

Fire and Flood

In 1881 and again in 1882 fire destroyed the fairground and building.

The board rebuilt the fairground, which a flood promptly destroyed in 1883

The board rebuilt 48 stalls, the barn and fine art hall in time for the fair

History of the Dearborn County Fair and 4-H

An example of some of the programs from the 1883 Dearborn County Fair Program:

Gus Sun Rodeo

Tumbling Arabs

The Singing Cowboys

Goat Races

Doll Baby Parade

Baby Show

Lamy's Hight Casting Act

Rio Grande Rangers

Ramond's Contortion Act

Rajah Troupe

The admission was 25 cents.

Visitors could also inspect a Case farm tractor exhibit. A company representative was in attendance to conduct demonstrations and answer questions. Equipment included tractors, cultivators, hay loaders and manure spreaders.

During the goat race, the goats were hitched to carts driven by young boys. The fairground was near the Ohio River. Another popular event was a Rooster Corn Eating Contest. The rooster that consumed the most corn during the contest won a prize for its boy or girl owner.

Victor Oberting sponsored parades with goats, horses, dogs and entertainers.

A nurse was in attendance at the rest rooms

Visitors got their drinking water from the town pump, used a tin cup.

In 1890 the Lawrenceburg Agricultural Society transferred ownership to the Lawrenceburg Fair Association. The Association took a ten year lease on the fairgrounds.

Lawrenceburg had no fair for eight years - 1882 - 1890

The Lawrenceburg Fair Association formed in 1890 and ran fairs for eighteen years

1894 Lawrenceburg Fair

August 22 - 25

Dearborn County had constructed a horse racing track that led the Chicago Times to announce, "racing by fast steppers on the finest half mile track in the state." The Times stated that they would announce the fair activities at a later date. During this era railroads and river boats offered special excursion rates out to the county fairs in rural communities.

Fair activities included:

Balloon Races

Bicycle Races

Horse racing, including trotting and running

In addition there were fruit, vegetable and flower displays from local farmers.

From a Fair Program for the August 26 1897 Fair

Cooks Mammoth Hippodrome

Riderless Horse Race

Steeple Chase Race

Standing Jockey Race

Bucking Horses

Chariot Races

Hurdle Races

Hound VS Horse Race

Running Team Race

Roman Standing Race

In 1897 Harrison organized its own fair, which they held in West Harrison for three years. A flood of the Whitewater River damaged the fairgrounds and the fair abandoned.

Indianapolis News reported on October 25, 1898

The Lawrenceburg Fair Board sold the fairgrounds to Victor Oberting, owner of the Garnier Oberting Brewing Company. The fair had been profitable when "hoochie coochie shows ran during the fair on the fairgrounds. An attempt by Oberting to clean up the fair resulted in a financial loss, leading Oberting to sell his shares, after which the fair would resume its previous programs.

Angola Herald August 27, 1902, page 13

The Lawrenceburg Fair Association formed in 1890 with William H. O'Brien as president, Victor Oberting as vice president.

Fair attendance averaged 12,000 - 15,000 and took in between $2000 - $2400 in ticket sales. The city owned the fairgrounds, which found use as a park during the time the fair was not in session.

The 1902 Dearborn County Fair Program included

Dearborn County Rough Riders Parade with 10 companies of Rough Riders

the 2000 troops would reenact the Battle of San Juan Hill

A military band also performed

Annie Oakly

Buckskin Ben

Note - the Rough Riders organized in Boon County, Kentucky and Dearborn County, Jacob Spanagel Barret commander

1903 Fair

Interchangeable buggy and road wagons on display

1908 fair attendance was 15,000 people. Street cars bound from Harrison and Aurora were so full that men hung from the cow catchers on the front and rear of the cars.

1911

White and colored baby contests

There were no fairs during 1918, 1919, 1920

1922 fair admission 50 cents

August 23 - 26

American Legion members free

1/2 mile mule race

County Road Race

Baby show

Horse races - most purses $200

Prizes awarded for the best

Vegetables,

Horse

Beef

Hog

July 28, 1934 Dearborn County Register

Congress of Daredevils

Famous Actress Crashes through wall

Feature of Thrill Day

Stock car driven 40 MPH into a a wall

Mary Wiggins actress to participate in the crash

40,000 expected attendance

Ash Can Derby

Car Jump with Motorcycles

Rain Insurance Policy Expired July 28, 1934

Premium 63.60

Insurance Company of North America

Insured gate receipts loss from 1/10 inch of rain or mor also against sleet, hail and snow.

July 19, 1937 Dearborn County Register

Reported extensive flood damage from the Ohio River flood that year. The Secretary Building was gone, the Auto Shed had collapsed, the art building twisted and wrecked, the horse tables damaged.

Levee construction in 1941 took most of the fairground, forcing its relocation to its current location. Governor Shricker attended the dedication ceremony and gave an address. Thunderstorms cut the crowd

June 24, 2002 Lawrenceburg Journal Press reported

2 million dollar renovation project included speedway, grandstand and concession stand along with some other renovations.

In 1952 Billboard magazine selected the Dearborn County Fair as a typical county fair, Mrs. America visited the fair.

Activities during this period included:

Skating Smith - act included skating through a fifteen inch tunnel

Pat and Will Levold Equlibrists

Americas Greatest Slack Wire

Daily Aeroplane rides

Amusement Rides

Moral and Refined Entertainment

Fireworks - different show every night

Famous Savilla Trio

Acrobats

Comedians

Cotton Picking Trio

Dearborn County Band

5 horse races daily

1971 Amos Oberting organizes Dog Show

1994 Abner Hall constructed

The modern Dearborn County Fair has evolved into a fair that highlights the many talents of young 4-H students. The fair also features a number of traditional events that include tractor pulls, a queen contest, fashion review and other fun activities. The event list currently includes:

4-H Poultry Show

4-H Dog Show

Youth Livestock Judging Contest

Opening Ceremony

Frog Jump Contest

Poultry Cooking Demo

4-H Royalty Crowning

Blue Grass Tractor Show

4-H Rabbit Show

Demonstration and Public Speaking

Contest Read Creative Writing

]4-H Fashion Review

Robotics and 3D Printing Demo

Flower Show

1-2-3-4 Kids Cook

Pedal Tractor Pull

4-H Swine Show

Lawn Mower Race and Back Seat Driver Race

Pygmy Fiber Class and Dairy Goat Show

Pike Bake Off

Baby Contest

Peach Baking Contest

Lamb Cooking Demo

Fun Horse Show

4-H Sheep Show

4-H Horse and Pony Show

Small Animal Supreme Showmanship Contest

4-H Pocket Pet Show

Cat Show

Lawn and Garden Contest

Alpaca and Llama Show

Dairy Show

4-H Beef Heifer Show

4-H Market Beef Show

Steam Powered Recycling

Muddy Madness - Kids games in the mud

Beef Cooking Demo - Marcia Parcell

Pig in the Pen

4-H Pork Chop Dinner

4-H Livestock Sale

Rodeo

The 4-H Program list for Dearborn County includes the following topics:

Beef

Cats

Dairy

Dog

Goats

Horse & Pony

Llama/Alpaca

Pocket Pets

Poultry

Game Bird Division

Duck Division

Turkey Division

Poultry Illustrated

Talk

Rabbit

Sheep

Swine

Aerospace

Alfalfa

Aquatic Science

Arts

& Crafts, Model Building and Wearable Arts

Beekeeping

Bicycle

Cake Decorating

Cat Poster

Child Development

Collections

Computers

Consumer Clothing

Consumer Dairy

Consumer Meats (Pork, Beef, & Lamb)

Corn

Creative Writing

Dog Poster

Electric

Entomology

Fashion Revue

Floriculture

-Flowers

Foods

Forestry

Frugal Fashion

Garden

Genealogy

Geology

Gift Wrapping

Hay

Health

Home Environment

Horse Science

Junior Leaders

Lawn & Garden Tractor

Llama/Alpaca Poster/Craft

People In My World

Photography

Potato

Poultry Display Boards/Science Display

Rabbit Poster

Radio

Recycling - Repurposing Project

Recycling Science Fair Project

Robotics

Scrapbook

Sewing

Sewing For Fun and Others

Shooting Sports

Small Grains (Barley, Oats, Rye, Triticale, Wheat)

Small Engines

Soil & Water Conservation

Soybeans

Sportfishing

Sports

Strawberry

Tobacco

Tractor

Veterinary Science

Weather

Weeds

Welding-Electric Arc

Wildlife

Woodworking

Dearborn County Fairground

351 E Eads Pkwy

Lawrenceburg, IN 47025

812-926-1189

https://www.dearborncounty4h.com/

https://www.facebook.com/DearbornCounty4HandComm
unityFair/

Extension Office

812-926-1189

dearborncountyfair@yahoo.com

http://www.dearborncountyfair.com

https://extension.purdue.edu/Dearborn/pages/default.asp x

Dearborn County 4-H Website

Dearborn County Fire Departments

Aurora Volunteer Fire Department

Aurora city officials purchased the first fire engine in 1876 from Ahrens & Company, a fire equipment manufacturer from Cincinatti, Ohio. The city organized the Volunteer Fire Department during the same year, appointing Edwin Trester as the first fire chief. They purchased the single cylinder, horse drawn pumper engine on a subscription plan. The firemen solicited one third of the money for the down payment and the city paid the remainder. Thomas Gaff, a distiller located in Aurora, probably provided a substantial portion of the financing as the first engine, Aurora No. 1, bore his name on a brass name plate on the exhaust stack. Gaff also purchased the first fire bell, installed in the first fire department building on Importing Street, the Gaff Building. this bell was installed on January 19, 1877. The city council replaced this bell on March 19,1880. This bell cracked and was replaced and was replaced. The replacement remained in service until September 9, 1952 when an electric alarm system replaced it.

New Fire House

The City Council approved a contract for a new fire house on November 5, 1886 at 218 Third Street. This building was completed on October 21, 1887.

Second Pumper

The city purchased a second pumper engine in 1895 which they called the "Aurora".

Cisterns

During this era the city relied on cisterns for fire protection. Scattered strategically around the city a sprinkler wagon brought water in from the Ohio River to fill the cistern and sprinkle water on the city's dirt streets to settle the dust. The sprinkler wagons were pulled by two horses and had large water tanks on them.

Water Works

Aurora city officials approved plans for a new water works system to supply water to the town on January 25, 1894. This system, completed in 1903, provided more water pressure for the citizens and fire protection.

Disposing of the Pumpers

On September 27, 1904 the city removed the two pumpers from service, keeping them to use as spares until 1907. With the improved water pressure provided by the new water system, they no longer needed the pumping engines. They used horse drawn ladder wagons and hose wagons to fight fires.

Motorized Fire Engines

Horses continued pulling the hose and ladder wagons until 1918 when the city approved the purchase of a new Model "T" Ford truck chassis, with hose bed, ladders and a 40-gallon chemical tank. Since the purchase of this new equipment, the Aurora Volunteer Fire Department has continued to upgrade its equipment, training and trucks.

Aurora Volunteer Fire Department

5950 Dutch Hollow Rd.

Aurora, IN

812-926-1682

http://aurora.in.us/fire-department.html

Lawrenceburg Fire Department

The founder of the A. D. Cook Company, A. D. Cook, founded the Lawrenceburg Fire Department in 1882. Composed of both full time and part time firefighters. the Lawrenceburg Fire Department provides fire and rescue service to the city of Lawrenceburg. The department added the Lawrenceburg Emergency Rescue service in 1951, using volunteer staff. The Rescue Service now has full time personnel on duty 24 hours a day.

Lawrenceburg Fire Department

300 W. Tate St

Lawrenceburg, IN

812-537-1509

https://www.thinklawrenceburg.com/government/depart ments/fire-department/

Dillsboro Volunteer Fire Department

Prior to 1888 Dillsboro citizens formed bucket brigades to fight fires. In 1888 the town purchased a hand pumper wagon. When a fire broke out local volunteers pulled the wagon by hand to the scene of the fire and used the hand powered pump to pump water on the fire. The town replaced this hand powered pumping engine sometime in the 1920's when it purchased a Dodge fire truck. The first organized volunteer fire department formed in 1927. The department used the old school building, built in 1905, as a fire station, using the old school bell as a fire bell. This building also housed the Town Hall. The Dillsboro Volunteer Fire Department reorganized in 1934. The town purchased a Chevrolet pumper truck in 1936. Sometime in the 1930's the Fire Department purchased a tract of land and installed playground equipment and sports fields. They constructed a concession stand and sold refreshment to those attending the various events and games at the park, using the profits to fund the fireman's treasury. They also sponsored an annual carnival at the park. In 1969 the Fire Department sold the park and used the proceeds to partially fund the construction of a new firehouse, which was dedicated at a ceremony on July 6, 1974.

Dillsboro Volunteer Fire Department

10100 Front St

Dillsboro, Indiana 47018

(812) 432-5262

https://dillsboro.in/fire-department/fire-department

https://www.facebook.com/DVFDIndiana/

Bright Volunteer Fire Department

The Bright Volunteer Fire Department was founded on July 28, 1948.

Bright Volunteer Fire Department

23759 Brightwood Dr

Lawrenceburg, IN 47025

812-637-3473

https://www.facebook.com/BrightFireDepartment/?rf=534263723416124

Moore's Hill- Sparta Volunteer Fire Department

16907 Manchester St

Comment [PW]:

Moore's Hill , In 47032

812-744-3787

mooreshillfire@seidata.com

https://www.facebook.com/Moores-Hill-Sparta-Township-Volunteer-Fire-Ems-191786227507182/

Saint Leon Volunteer Fire Department

28885 St Joe Dr

West Harrison, IN 47060

(812) 576-3450

https://www.facebook.com/stleonfire/

Dearborn County Libraries

Aurora Public Library District

Dillsboro Public Library

Lawrenceburg Public Library

North Dearborn Branch Library

25969 Dole Road

West Harrison, IN 47060

North Dearborn Branch Library

Local History Library @ The Depot

510 Second Street

Aurora, Indiana 47001

Aurora Public Library District

For more on the Aurora Library see the article in the National Register of Historic Places – Aurora Downtown.

Aurora Public Library District

414 Second Street

Aurora, IN 47001

Aurora Public Library District

https://eapld.org/

Dillsboro Public Library

10151 Library Lane

Dillsboro, Indiana 47018

Local History Library @ The Depot

Aurora, Indiana 47001

Lawrenceburg Public Library District

For more on the Lawrenceburg Library see the article in the National Register of Historic Places – Lawrenceburg Downtown.

Lawrenceburg Public Library District

150 Mary Street

Lawrenceburg, IN 47025

Lawrenceburg Public Library District

https://www.lpld.lib.in.us

lawplib@lpld.lib.in.us

Dearborn County Auto Trails

Indiana's Historic Pathways

The Indiana Historic Pathway travels through sixteen counties from the Wabash River to the Ohio River. The Trail follows the path of the Buffalo Trace and passes dozens of historic spots and parks in southern Indiana. Attractions include historic mansions, museums, caves, antiques, and much more. the tour also includes two Indiana State Historic Sites, two National Wildlife Refuges, state parks and churches. Counties include:

Clark County

Crawford County

Daviess County

Dearborn County

Dubois County

Floyd County

Harrison County

Jackson County

Jennings County

Knox County

Lawrence County

Martin County

Orange County

Pike County

Ripley County

Washington County

For more information, contact:

Historic Southern Indiana

University of Southern Indiana

8600 University Boulevard

Evansville, IN 47712

(812) 465-7013

(800) 489-4474

hsi@usi.edu

Historic Southern Indiana

University of Southern Indiana

8600 University Boulevard

Evansville, IN 47712

Phone: (812) 465-7013

Toll free: (800) 489-4474

E-mail: hsi@usi.edu

http://www.usi.edu/ihp/index.aspx

John Hunt Morgan Heritage Trail 1863

On July 8, 1863, Confederate General John Hunt Morgan crossed the Ohio River at Brandenburg, Kentucky and invaded Indiana. His army consisted of two thousand cavalrymen. His purpose was to divert Union General Ambrose Burnside's Army of the Ohio in eastern Tennessee and make them come north.

Morgan's Raiders, as the small army came to be known, spent six days pillaging, looting and burning across seven southern Indiana counties before crossing the state line and invading Ohio. Morgan tried to cross the Ohio River at Buffington Island. Union gunboats and forces intercepted him. Some of his force managed to escape into West Virginia and about 750 were captured. Morgan and about 300 men fled into northeastern Ohio. They were captured near West Point Ohio on July 26.

In Indiana Morgan's Raid crossed Harrison, Washington, Scott, Jennings, Jefferson, Ripley and Dearborn counties.

The Indiana portion of the raid has been mapped into an Auto Tour. The John Hunt Morgan Heritage Trail traces the route of Morgan's Raiders through Indiana as it fled through the countryside into Ohio.

John Hunt Morgan Heritage Trail

1981 S. Industrial Park Road, Ste. 1

PO Box 407

Versailles, IN 47042

hhhills@seidata.com

812-689-4107

http://www.hhhills.org/JohnHuntMorgan.html

Ohio River Scenic Byway Driving Tour

Scenic Byway – Southern Indiana Drive

Drive the 302 miles of scenic beauty along the Ohio River in Southern Indiana. The Ohio River Scenic Byway goes through historic communities, national forests and quaint villages. This wonderful drive through southern Indiana is a wonderful experience and allows you to visit all the wonderful places in southern Indiana. The tour passes through historic river towns like New Albany, Clarksburg, Madison, Vevay and Aurora. Tour historic mansions, state parks and visit antique shops along the way. Many wonderful restaurants inhabit the towns along the way, as well as quaint shops, galleries and museums.

On its way across the state, it crosses Clark County, Crawford County, Dearborn County, Floyd County, Harrison County, Jefferson County, Ohio County, Perry County, Posey County, South Central Indiana, Spencer County, Switzerland County, Vanderburgh County, and Warrick County.

For more information, contact:

Historic Southern Indiana

University of Southern Indiana

8600 University Blvd.

Evansville, In 47712

Tel: 812-465-7013

Tollfree: 800-489-4474

Fax: 812: 465-7061

E-mail: hsi@usi.edu

http://ohioriverbyway.com/

The Dearborn County Visitor Center conducts a number of group tours. These include:

Dine with History in Southeast Indiana - Taste of Southeast Indiana

Fall Mums, Farms & Markets

Christmas Crumpets & Evergreen Boughs

This is just a sampling, for a current list and contact information:

Dearborn County Visitor Center

320 Walnut Street

Lawrenceburg, IN 47025

812-537-0814

800-322-8198

dearborn@visitsoutheastindiana.com

https://www.visitsoutheastindiana.com

Group   Tours   -
https://www.visitsoutheastindiana.com/tour-southeast-
indiana

Windows of Aurora Murals

This walking tour allows visitors to walk around downtown
Aurora to see the sixty-four murals painted on windows. A
brochure that explains the murals is available at this link:

http://aurora.in.us/mainstreet.html

Apple users can download an ap that makes this tour an
interactive event.

Dearborn County Historic Bridges

Guilford Covered Bridge

See Historic Marker Listing

Collier Ridge Road Arch Bridge

Dearborn County Bridge 54

Collier Ridge Road Over Branch West Fork Tanners Creek

Concrete Closed Spandrel Deck Arch, Fixed Length: 49 ft

Main Span: 42.3 ft

George Street Bridge

See National Register Listing

Guilford Red Bridge

Collier Ridge Road Bridge

Collier Ridge Road Over West Fork Tanners Creek

Metal 7 Panel Rivet-Connected Pratt Through Truss, Fixed Length: 138.8 ft

Main Span: 135.5 ft

Roadway: 12.8 ft

Main Spans: 1 Built 1915

This beautiful former railroad bridge is slated for demolition but community residents want to see this historic bridge rehabilitated.

Laughery Creek Road Bridge

Laughery Creek Road (Abandoned Alignment) Over Laughery Creek Branch

Metal 3 Panel Rivet-Connected Warren Pony Truss, Fixed Length: 41 ft

Main Span: 39 ft

Roadway: 15.7 ft

Main Spans: 1

Built 1917

This small pony truss has been bypassed and abandoned and is noted for decorative finials on its railings.

Lost Bridge

Dearborn County Bridge 15,

Ohio County Bridge 29

Belles Branch Road Over Laughery Creek

Metal 8 Panel Pin-Connected Pratt Through Truss, Fixed Length: 147 ft

Main Span: 141.7 ft

Roadway: 16.7 ft

Main Spans: 1

Built 1916

By: Oregonia Bridge Company of Lebanon, Ohio This bridge may be so named because anyone who has discovered this awe-inspiring bridge in the middle of nowhere was lost!

Triple Whipple Bridge

See National Register of Historic Places listing

Dearborn County 1938 U.S. 50 Bridge Over Tanners Creek

31 ton weight limit

three-lane bridge currently operated as one-way eastbound bridge;

five spans (81'-3", 105'-7.5", 113'-9", 105'-7.5", 81'-3").

This bridge is eligible for listing in the National Register of Historic Places,

https://www.in.gov/indot/2919.htm

Phantom Bridge On The Old Trackville Ghost Road, St. Leon, Indiana

Built in 1910 this steel pony truss bridge is now considered a Phantom Bridge as it's located on a Ghost Road. A rare structure that few people have ever seen

The Railroad Trestle That Outlasted John Hunt Morgan, Bonnell, Indiana

Dearborn County Waterways

Hogan Creek

Length - About 1900 feet

North Hogan and South Hogan Creeks come together near the intersection of West Side Drive and US 50 in downtown Aurora. A short distance after passing under bridges for US 50 and George Street, Hogan Creek empties into the Ohio River.

Townships

Center

North Hogan Creek

Length - Approximately 18.4 miles

In Dearborn County - Approximately 16 Miles

North Hogan Creek begins in northeastern Ripley County near County Road 800 E about .5 miles south of its intersection with Indiana State Road 101.It flows through south central Dearborn County on a northwest to southeast incline. It drains approximately 19,000 acres in Ripley County and 63,000 acres in Dearborn County. About 47% of the watershed is agricultural land, 45% woodland and the remainder city land or water.

Townships

Center

North Hogan Road, accessed from Indiana State Road 48 about 1 mile from the Ripley County/Dearborn County line, follows most of Hogan Creeks course.

It intersects South Hogan Creek in Aurora, crosses US Route 50 and enters the Ohio River. These boating facilities are located near the mouth of Hogan Creek:

Sunset Bay Marina

799 Westside Drive (SR 350)

Aurora, IN 47001

513-266-1117

Hogan Creek Canoe Ramp

Waterways Park

Aurora, IN 47001

Hogan Creek Watershed

http://www.dearborncountywatersheds.org/Hogan-Creek.html

South Hogan Creek

Length - About 25.5 miles

South Hogan Creek begins in Ripley County near County Road 500 E about .3 miles south of Indiana State Road 350 near the town of Milan. It flows generally southeast approximately 7.5 miles to the Ripley/Dearborn County line just south of Moore's Hill. From the county line South Hogan Creek flows approximately 14 miles to its confluence with Hogan Creek.

Hogan Creek intersects County Road 300N, E CR 200 N, CR Road 525 E, CR 625 E, Indiana State Road 101 in Ripley County. After crossing into Dearborn County it crosses Boyd Road, County Line Road, Birchwood Lane, Lauman Road, Station Hollow Road, Lower Dillsboro Road before joining North Hogan Creek shortly before it empties into the Ohio River.

In Ripley County Milan Creek is the main tributary. In Dearborn County Whitaker Creek, Long Branch and Allen Branch are the main tributaries that empty into South Hogan Creek.

South Hogan Creek is flanked by South Hogan Road, Chesterville Road and Lower Dillsboro Road.

Townships – Center

Tanners Creek - East Fork

Length - About 14 miles

The east fork of Tanner's Creek begins east of Lawrenceville Road south of Lawrenceburg, Indiana. First flowing north, the east fork turns east, then southeast to meet the West Fork of Tanners Creek at Guilford, Indiana. On the way it intersects Indiana State Road 46, St. Peter's Road, SR 46 as it turns southeast, North Dearborn Road and Yorkridge Road. Indiana State Road 1 paralells its course after it meets Slab Camp Creek. Tributaries include Turkey Run, Ennis Creek, Slab Camp Creek, Brushy Creek before joining the West Fork to form Tanners Creek.

Tanners Creek - West Fork

Length - About 11 miles

The West Fork begins south of North Dearborn Road between Van Wedding and Weisburg Roads. Flowing generally southeast, the West Fork intersects Weisburg Road, Ester Ridge Road, Creekside Drive, Konradi Road, Villa Lane, Collier Lane, before meeting the East Fork at Guilford, where they form Tanners Creek. Tributaries include Taylor Creek, Leatherwood Creek, Ziegler Creek, Norton Run, Fox Run, The West Fork is bounded first by Creekside Drive and Bonnell Road. Guilford Bridge Park is located at the junction. It is bounded by Cook Road and Indiana State Road 1 during much of its course. Towns located along the West Fork include Weisburg and Guilford.

Tanners Creek

Length - About 11.5 Miles

Tanner's Creek begins at the junction of the East and West Forks on the eastern edge of Guilford in southeastern Dearborn County. Flowing generally southeast, Tanners Creek intersects Kaiser Drive, Pribble Road, US Route 50 before emptying into the Ohio River. Indiana State Road 1 follows its course over much of its journey in Dearborn County. Tanner Avenue and Schenley Place hug its bank in Greendale while Industrial Drive follows it in Lawrenceburg.

Tanners Creek drains nearly 68,000 acres consisting of almost all crop or forest land.

Tanners Public Boat Dock

U.S. 50

Tanners Creek Ln.

Lawrenceburg, Ind.

Tanners Creek Watershed

http://www.dearborncountywatersheds.org/Tanners-
Creek.html

The boat dock is accessible from US 50 near Tanners Creek
confluence with the Ohio River.

Laughery Creek

Laughery Creek is about ninety miles long, beginning in
Ripley County. As it exits Ripley County, it forms the
boundary of Ohio and Dearborn Counties. Laughery Creek
receives its name from Revolutionary War Colonel
Archibald Lochry, who died with many of his company
along the banks of the creek on August 24, 1781. Laughery
Creek drains the majority of Ripley County. Its source is
southeast of Napoleon, in the northwest corner of the
County, and exits the county near Friendship, in the
southeast corner. The Laughery Creek valley serves as the
basin for Versailles Lake in Versailles State Park. The
Busching Covered Bridge spans Laughery Creek just south
of the Park. It is still an active bridge.

Laughery Creek in Ripley County

Length - About 50 Miles

Flowing first north, Laughery bends around and flows
generally southeast through the midsection of Ripley
County. On its way it intersects US Route 421 twice,
Milhousen Road, County Road 1050 N, 350 W, 250 W, 1150
N, 200 W, Indiana State Road 229, CR 1000 N, Indiana State
Road 48, Mud Pike Road, Indiana State Road 350, County

Road 25 S, US Route 50, County Road 250 S, South Cave Hill Road (twice), Indiana State Road 62 before passing into Dearborn County just east of Friendship. Cave Hill Road follows much of its course below its intersection with Signor Hill Road. Chief tributaries of Laughery include Tub Creek, Walnut Fork, Little Laughery, Ripley Creek, Castators Creek, Goose Creek, Raccoon Creek, Caeser Creek.

Laughery Creek passes close to the Ripley County Towns of Napoleon, Osgood, Versailles and Friendship. The majority of the Laughery Creek valley in Ripley County is heavily forested and provides excellent farmland on the flat bottomlands that border its banks. Its major tributary, Little Laughery, flows from Batesville, Indiana in the north. The junction of the two Laugheries is just southeast of Ballstown, Indiana on Indiana State Road 229. Other tributaries of Laughery Creek in Ripley County include Plum Creek and Ripley Creek.

In Ripley County Laughery Creek flows through Versailles State Park.

Laughery Creek in Dearborn County

Length - About 25 miles

Laughery Creek enters Dearborn County from Ripley County about 1.75 miles southeast of Friendship, Indiana and exits into the Ohio River near Aurora, Indiana. Riverview Cemetery is on the east bank of Laughery Creek. It is the approximate scene of "Lochrey's Massacre." The cemetery is located on East Laughery Creek Road, just off Indiana State Road 56.

An historic bridge, a triple-intersection Pratt truss, also known as the Triple Whipple Bridge, crosses Laughery Creek near its junction with the Ohio River. The bridge was constructed in 1878. It was restored in 2008.

Laughery Creek in Ohio County

Length - About 25 miles

Laughery Creek forms the northern border separating Ohio and Dearborn Counties. From the east, East Laughery Creek Road runs alongside Laughery Creek for about 4.65 miles from its intersection with Indiana State Road 56 near Riverview Cemetery. Cole Lane and Nelson Road from Ohio County make up the north and south roads meeting at this intersection. Here, East Laughery Road becomes Laughery Road, which winds along the creek for another 1.65 miles, where it meets Huseman Road. See the Huesman Road article to see the details of this road. After the Huesman Road and Indiana State Road 262 intersection, West Laughery Creek Road branches off from SR 262 and winds west along the creek for for about 8.11 miles to its intersection with Bell's Branch Road. Bell's Branch continues south into Ohio County and north to an intersection with Nolte Road. On its way, generally southwest, West Laughery Creek Road intersects Arlington Road, Roberts Road, Prosperity Ridge Road, Baum Hollow Road, Milton Bear Branch Road and Hartford Pike roughly parellel Laughery Creek in Ohio County.

From west to east, Laughery tributaries in Dearborn County include Bob Branch, Mud Lick and Goodpasture Branch.

Townships

Center

Whitewater River

Length in Indiana - About seventeen miles.

The union of the East and West Forks of the Whitewater River in Franklin County a little southwest of Brookville, Indiana forms the Whitewater River. The West Fork rises in Randolph County, the East in Wayne County. The Whitewater River crosses Franklin and Dearborn Counties before exiting the State of Indiana and entering Ohio.The river valley's watershed is steep, creating the swiftest river in Indiana as it falls an average of six feet per mile. The swift water affords some excellent canoeing opportunities along most of its length.

Whitewater River In Franklin County

Brookville Lake contains the waters of the east Fork of the Whitewater River and forms most of that branch in Franklin County. The East Fork flows about two miles from the dam's spillway to its junction with the West Fork on the southwest corner of Brookville. The west fork of the Whitewater River enters Franklin County about two miles north of Laurel, Indiana a short distance east of Indiana State Road 121. The West Fork flows approximately sixteen miles to its union with the east Fork near Brookville. Indiana State Road 121 connects Laurel, in Franklin County, and Connersville, in Fayette County. US Route 52 follows the course of the Whitewater River over most of its course until the river enters Dearborn County. Towns along the course of the river include Brookville, Mound Haven, and Cedar Grove. Towns along the West Branch include Laurel and Yellow Bank.

Whitewater River In Dearborn County

Length - About 7.71 miles

The Whitewater River enters Dearborn County about 9.75 miles southeast of the junction of the East and West Forks in Franklin Counties. About 3 miles southeast of the county line, it passes under Interstate 74 and Indiana State Road 46. The Whitewater River passes out of Dearborn County and into Ohio about 4.55 miles east of this intersection.

There is one canoe trip in Dearborn County on this streatch of the Whitewater River. It begins in Franklin, County near Laurel at Whitewater Canal Feeder Dam at Laurel. This park is located on Dam Road on the east side of the Whitewater River. To get to Dam Road from Indiana State Road 121, go east on Pearl Street. You will cross the Whitewater River. Dam Road is the first road to the right after you cross the river. There is a small park on the right side of the road about one mile from the intersection.

Barber follows the course of the west bank of the Whitewater from its intersection with St. Peter's Road in Franklin County to its intersection with Indiana State Road 46 in Dearborn County. Pinhook Road follows the river at three spots from its western terminus on White's Hill Road to its southern terminus on North Dearborn Road near the Indiana/Ohio State Line. Old State Road 52 comes close to the Whitewater River in two places and crosses it near its southern terminus at an intersection with North Dearborn Road near the Indiana/Ohio State Line.

McCann Creek and Pinhook Creek are tributaries of the Whitewater River in Franklin County.

The take out point is a bridge which crosses the Whitewater River on the Indiana State Line near the intersection of State Street, Campbell Road and Jameson Road in West Harrison, Indiana. This is a 26 mile, nine hour canoe trip and is very popular in the summer months so the river may be crowded. There are canoe liveries in the area which rent canoes over this stretch of water.

The Indiana Department of Natural Resources has compiled a plethora of information about canoeing opportunities along the Whitewater River. To see this information about the Whitewater river, click the link.

http://www.in.gov/dnr/outdoor/4473.htm

Great Miami River

The Great Miami River is in the state of Ohio for the vast majority of its length. The final half mile or so is in Dearborn County, just east of Lawrenceburg. The mouth of the river is in Ohio, but one channel does enter the Ohio River in Indiana. The Great Miami River actually snakes into Indiana twice. It enters, flowing northwest, then turns back east and reenters Ohio for a short time and then turns southwest entering Indiana for the last time. The river then turns southeast, enters Ohio and finally pours its waters into the Ohio River. All of this happens inside the Interstate 275 loop.

A protected wetlands area, the Oxbow, is located along the Great Miami River east of Lawrenceburg.

Ohio River

Total River Miles - 981.1 mi

The Ohio River forms at the junction of the Allegheny and Monongahela Rivers in southwestern Pennsylvania. The river forms the boundaries of West Virginia, Ohio, Indiana, Kentucky and Illinois before emptying into the Mississippi River near Cairo, Illinois.

Tributaries of the Ohio River

Allegheny River – Pittsburgh, Pennsylvania

Monongahela River – Pittsburgh

Beaver River – Rochester, Pennsylvania

Little Muskingum River – Ohio

Muskingum River – Marietta, Ohio

Little Kanawha River – Parkersburg, West Virginia

Hocking River – Hockingport, Ohio

Kanawha River – Point Pleasant, West Virginia

Guyandotte River – Huntington, West Virginia

Big Sandy River – Kentucky-West Virginia border

Little Sandy River – Greenup, Kentucky

Little Scioto River – Sciotoville, Ohio

Scioto River – Portsmouth, Ohio

Kinniconick Creek – Vanceburg, Kentucky

Little Miami River – Cincinnati, Ohio

Licking River – Newport-Covington, Kentucky

Great Miami River – Ohio-Indiana border

Kentucky River – Carrollton, Kentucky

Salt River – West Point, Kentucky

Green River – near Henderson, Kentucky

Wabash River – Indiana-Illinois-Kentucky border

Saline River – Illinois

Cumberland River – Smithland, Kentucky

Tennessee River – Paducah, Kentucky

Cache River – Illinois

Ohio River in Indiana
Total River Miles - 357
From River Mile 491.34 to River Mile 848
Ohio River In Dearborn County
Length - About 7.36 Miles
Parks along the Ohio River
Lesko Ohio River Park
Aurora, Indiana

Dearborn County Towns along the River
Aurora,
Lawrenceburg

Dearborn County Hiking/Biking Trails along the Ohio River
River Trail
Dearborn Trail

Indiana State Highways along the River

Indiana State Road 56

Dearborn County Marinas
Blue Ribbon Marina
Ohio River Access

Westside Drive

Aurora

(812)-926-0830

Lischgke Boat Harbor

Ohio River Access

Judiciary Street

Aurora

(812)-926-0553

Aurora Landing

103 Judiciary Street

Aurora, IN 47001

812-926-1774

Aurora Marina & Campground

11598 State Route 56

Aurora, IN 47001

812-926-2150

Hogan Creek Canoe Ramp

Waterways Park

Aurora, IN 47001

Holiday Hills Resort & Marina

4600 Hartford Pike

Aurora IN, 47001

812-926-2331

Lighthouse Point Yacht Club

11042 State Route 56

Aurora, IN 47001

812-926-4505

Sunset Bay Marina

799 Westside Drive (SR 350)

Aurora, IN 47001

513-266-1117

Tradewinds Marina

605 Green Boulevard

Aurora, IN 47001

812-926-0341

Tanners Public Boat Dock

U.S. 50

Tanners Creek Ln.

Lawrenceburg, Ind.

Dearborn County Time Line

Aug. 24, 1781 - Lochry's Defeat

1794 - First Settlers

1799 - Kibbey's Road

1798 - Israel Ludlow Surveys True Meridian That Became Indiana/Ohio State Line

April 06, 1801 - Land Office in Cincinnati Began Selling Land

April 9, 1801 - Joseph Hayes made the first recorded land purchase in Dearborn County

July 23, 1801 - Samuel Vance Purchases the Land that Became Lawrenceburg

March 7, 1803 - William Henry Harrison organized Dearborn County

1803 - The first court took place in September

1810 - The First Court House

1811 - Franklin County was separated from Dearborn County in

1835 - the county seat to be moved from Lawrenceburg to Wilmington in

1804 - The first Dearborn County jail was built .

1813 - West Harrison

1818 - Ripley County Seperated from Dearborn County

1819 - Aurora Platted

1819 - First Ohio River Ferry

1828 - The "Second" Court House

1830 - Dillsboro

1839 - Moore's Hill

1844 - County Seat Returns to Lawrenceburg

1844 - The Third Court House

1844 - Ohio County was created and separated from Dearborn County

1852 - Stephen Ludlow platted Greendale

June 15, 1870 - Current Court House

1887 - George Street Bridge

1887 - Aurora City Hall

1894 - Lawrenceburg Fair

1913 - Aurora Public Library District

1915 - Lawrenceburg Public Library;

1937 - Ohio River Flood

1970 - Hidden Valley Lake.

Indiana County – Back Road Numbering System

Indiana uses a system of numbering its back roads which on the surface appears confusing, but is really quite logical, once you understand the basics of how it works. Most, but not all, counties use the same basic road numbering system. Most of the counties which do not use it have very hilly terrain which renders the grid system useless for their needs. Most of these counties utilize a naming system which has no basis in geographic placement, as the grid system used by most other counties.

Think of the county road system as a grid, as pictured in the drawing. The center of this system is usually the county seat, which in most, but not all, counties is close to the geographic center of the county. Notice the two black lines. The north/south axis is called the base and the east/west axis is called the baseline. Thus any point on the road called Base Road is going to be either directly north, or south, of the geographic center located in the county seat. This is usually the court house. Any location on Baseline Road is going to be directly east or west of the county seat.

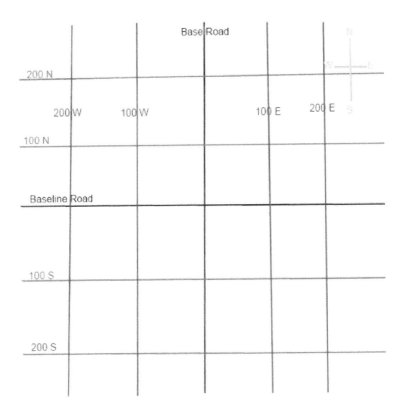

Miles are divided into hundreds. N and S roads are indicated by the red lines. 100 N means the road is one mile north of the baseline. 200 N is two miles north of the baseline. Similarly, 100 S would be one mile south of the baseline, and 200 S two miles south. 1200 S would be twelve miles south of the baseline. 750 N would be seven and one half miles north of the baseline and 725 N would be seven and a quarter north of the baseline.

The East and West roads, indicated by the blue lines are exactly the same as the red lined North and South roads, with each division of 100 equaling one mile.

```
                              |Base Road
                              |
                              |
────────────────────────────|200N──────────────────────
                              |
                              |
                              |100N
────────────────────────────|──────────────────────────
                              |
                              |
─────Baseline Road───────────|──────────────────────────
                              |
                              |
                              |100S
────────────────────────────|──────────────────────────
                              |
                              |
                              |200S
────────────────────────────|──────────────────────────
                              |
                              |
```

It is important to remember that the designation N, E, S, or W does not indicate which direction the road travels. It designates the direction that the road lies in relation to either the Base or Baseline roads. Thus an E or W road always travels with a north/south orientation, and N and S roads always have an east/west orientation. Since counties all use their own numbering system, a road will almost always change numbers when you cross a county line. Thus 500 N in one county may become 1200 N in the next one over.

Addresses of homes and businesses may be located using this system, as the home numbering system corresponds to the county road numbers. A home address of 1055 N County Road 500E would be located .055 mile north of County Road 100 N on County Road 500 E. 12355 E County Road 700 N would be .355 miles east of County Road 1200 E.

Using the road grid numbering system you can navigate around the county and find home and business addresses quickly and easily on a map once you understand the system.

Acknowledgements

April 06, 1801 - Land Office in Cincinnati Began Selling Land

People, Industries and Institutions ...

By Archibald Shaw

P 116

https://books.google.com/books?id=c080AQAAMAAJ&pg=PA115&lpg=PA115&dq=dearborn+county+%22surveys%22+indiana+1801&source=bl&ots=A76uyx3rgB&sig=ACfU3U1JjjSbEZJ2kF_vRbIVLf9sQczcAg&hl=en&sa=X&ved=2ahUKEwilgKPWpaLsAhXEWM0KHdJAAd84ChDoATAHegQICBAC#v=onepage&q=dearborn%20county%20%22surveys%22%20indiana%201801&f=false

https://www.tribstar.com/community/genealogy-learning-about-indianas-gore-area/article_2e86b5bc-576a-5265-9145-3e986b8907ae.html

https://books.google.com/books?id=gDjMG4HV91kC&pg=PA34&lpg=PA34&dq=rufus+putnam+survey+%221797%22&source=bl&ots=gjFd5I8GxH&sig=ACfU3U1Bb8Oujuxiq83iHnrE5-49Us0BfQ&hl=en&sa=X&ved=2ahUKEwiR8NPYheflAhVBPawKHYLbA9YQ6AEwCHoECAgQAQ#v=onepage&q=rufus%20putnam%20survey%20%221797%22&f=false

1798- Isreal Ludlow Surveys True Meridian That Became Indiana/Ohio State Line

American Boundaries: The Nation, the States, the Rectangular Survey

By Bill Hubbard

https://books.google.com/books?id=LMacwod5KLwC&pg=PA254&lpg=PA254&dq=ludlow+1798+meridian+indiana+ohio+border&source=bl&ots=WN3BCmEOHQ&sig=ACfU3U0MynFP-3clKD6DvvT_xnITYzQjJg&hl=en&sa=X&ved=2ahUKEwihoubds_HmAhWOGM0KHeBrDCMQ6AEwAHoECAoQAQ#v=onepage&q=ludlow%201798%20meridian%20indiana%20ohio%20border&f=false

Dearborn County History

http://www.dearborncounty.org/category/subcategory.php?categoryid=17

http://en.wikipedia.org/wiki/Dearborn_County,_Indiana

http://genealogytrails.com/ind/dearborn/history.html

Henry Dearborn (Feb. 23, 1751-June 6, 1829)

https://en.wikipedia.org/wiki/Henry_Dearborn

http://www.seacoastonline.com/news/20180621/story-of-general-henry-dearborn

Revolutionary War Journals of Henry Dearborn, 1775-1783

By Henry Dearborn

https://books.google.com/books?id=dUBt7zJodLEC&pg=PA48&lpg=PA48&dq=henry+dearborn+enlists+1775&source=bl&ots=ZQgzssayOb&sig=d8gWIChpXlN8QFLMm6loFg26AOw&hl=en&sa=X&ved=2ahUKEwj0o6XN-

NPeAhWqooMKHfoxDTkQ6AEwCHoECAEQAQ#v=onepage&q=henry%20dearborn%20enlists%201775&f=false

https://www.geni.com/people/Maj-Gen-Henry-Dearborn-US-Secretary-of-War/6000000009858101089

Dearborn County Geography:

http://www.peakbagger.com/peak.aspx?pid=22959

Soil Survey of Dearborn and Ohio Counties - Allan K. Nickell

https://www.nrcs.usda.gov/Internet/FSE_MANUSCRIPTS/indiana/dearborn_ohioIN1981/dearborn.pdf

Townships

https://www.familysearch.org/wiki/en/Dearborn_County,_Indiana_Genealogy

Aurora, Indiana

https://en.wikipedia.org/wiki/Aurora,_Indiana

http://history.rays-place.com/in/db-aurora.htm

http://www.ingenweb.org/indearborn/Pages/Riverview_Cemetery.shtml

http://history.rays-place.com/in/db-aurora.htm

Saint Leon, Indiana

https://en.wikipedia.org/wiki/Saint_Leon,_Indiana

http://dearborncountydemocrats.com/poll-raising/

https://blog.newspapers.library.in.gov/the-democratic-emblem-the-rooster-started-in-indiana-in-1840-before-the-donkey-in-1870/

Bright, Indiana

http://indianaplaces.com/blog/2010/09/20/bright-indiana/

https://en.wikipedia.org/wiki/Bright,_Indiana

https://www.facebook.com/places/Things-to-do-in-Bright-Indiana/103751506330078/

Hidden Valley

https://en.wikipedia.org/wiki/Hidden_Valley,_Indiana

Bonnell

https://youtu.be/Dv4zRvIelvI

https://historyinyourownbackyard.com/video/ghost-town-of-bonnell-indiana/

Braysville

https://en.wikipedia.org/wiki/Braysville,_Indiana

Chesterville

https://en.wikipedia.org/wiki/Chesterville,_Indiana

Cochran

https://en.wikipedia.org/wiki/Cochran,_Indiana

History of Dearborn and Ohio Counties, Indiana: From Their Earliest ..

https://books.google.com/books?id=QpYh2LvF6BIC&pg=PA478&lpg=PA478&dq=center
+township+dearborn+county+indiana+named+for&source=bl&ots=nLntTCwOlv&sig=AC
fU3U09nhFNe_sadcdwHzft9IOpl_-
RTw&hl=en&sa=X&ved=2ahUKEwiuo5Wix9boAhWSXc0KHZ46DLk4FBDoATABegQIDB
Ao#v=onepage&q=center%20township%20dearborn%20county%20indiana%20named%20
for&f=false

Cold Springs

https://en.wikipedia.org/wiki/Cold_Springs,_Indiana

Farmers Retreat

https://en.wikipedia.org/wiki/Farmers_Retreat,_Indiana

https://www.lpld.lib.in.us/briefhistory

Hardinsburg

https://en.wikipedia.org/wiki/Hardinsburg,_Dearborn_County,_Indiana

Hubbells Corner

https://en.wikipedia.org/wiki/Hubbells_Corner,_Indiana

Kyle

https://en.wikipedia.org/wiki/Kyle,_Indiana

Lawrenceburg Junction

https://en.wikipedia.org/wiki/Lawrenceburg_Junction,_Indiana

Lawrenceville

https://en.wikipedia.org/wiki/Lawrenceville,_Indiana

Logan

https://en.wikipedia.org/wiki/Logan,_Dearborn_County,_Indiana

Manchester

https://en.wikipedia.org/wiki/Manchester,_Indiana

Mount Sinai

https://en.wikipedia.org/wiki/Mount_Sinai,_Indiana

New Alsace

https://en.wikipedia.org/wiki/New_Alsace,_Indiana

Sparta

https://en.wikipedia.org/wiki/Sparta,_Indiana

Weisburg

https://en.wikipedia.org/wiki/Weisburg,_Indiana

Utah

https://roadsidethoughts.com/in/utah-xx-dearborn-profile.htm

https://en.wikipedia.org/wiki/Utah,_Indiana

Wilmington

https://en.wikipedia.org/wiki/Wilmington,_Indiana

Wrights Corner

https://en.wikipedia.org/wiki/Wrights_Corner,_Indiana

George Street Bridge

https://en.wikipedia.org/wiki/George_Street_Bridge_(Aurora,_Indiana)

https://npgallery.nps.gov/AssetDetail/NRIS/84001012

Squire Whipple

http://scihi.org/squire-whipple/

https://en.wikipedia.org/wiki/Squire_Whipple

http://scihi.org/squire-whipple/

https://prabook.com/web/squire.whipple/1864952

Moore's Hill United Methodist Church

https://npgallery.nps.gov/AssetDetail/NRIS/97001537

https://en.wikipedia.org/wiki/Moores_Hill_United_Methodist_Church

St. John's Lutheran Church and School

http://www.usachurches.org/church/st-john-lutheran-church-and-school.htm

https://digital.library.in.gov/Record/IUPUI_IHAS-5219

Hamline Chapel United Methodist Church

https://npgallery.nps.gov/AssetDetail/NRIS/82000030

https://en.wikipedia.org/wiki/Hamline_Chapel_United_Methodist_Church

Levi Stevens House

https://npgallery.nps.gov/AssetDetail/NRIS/96000599

https://en.wikipedia.org/wiki/Levi_Stevens_House

Title of Marker

Lochry's Defeat

https://en.wikipedia.org/wiki/Archibald_Lochry

https://en.wikipedia.org/wiki/Lochry%27s_Defeat

Title of Marker:

Kibbey's Road

http://www.geni.com/people/Major-Ephraim-Kibbey/6000000019078556060

https://books.google.com/books?id=n6fmymuZjRwC&pg=PA43&lpg=PA43&dq=Kibbey
%27s+Road&source=bl&ots=zpl_xNLQYf&sig=VUGerT_94MmdMTsV6XgUCz5l7-
4&hl=en&sa=X&ved=0CDsQ6AEwB2oVChMI18WmodPsxwIVitCACh2Xegj8#v=onepage
&q=Kibbey's%20Road&f=false

https://books.google.com/books?id=_9UyAQAAMAAJ&pg=PA353&lpg=PA353&dq=Kib
bey%27s+Road&source=bl&ots=8qIu6bYJXJ&sig=WpPSOOvLF60Yz7gxvg7ZFKq5dIY&hl
=en&sa=X&ved=0CCwQ6AEwA2oVChMI18WmodPsxwIVitCACh2Xegj8#v=onepage&q=
Kibbey's%20Road&f=false

Title of Marker:

Greenville Treaty Line

https://en.wikipedia.org/wiki/Treaty_of_Greenville

http://www.u-s-history.com/pages/h1016.html

http://www.ohiohistorycentral.org/w/Treaty_of_Greeneville_(1795)?rec=1418

Title of Marker:

Canal Junction

http://www.ohiohistorycentral.org/w/Cincinnati_and_Whitewater_Canal?rec=682

http://www.indianamuseum.org/explore/whitewater-
canal?gclid=CjwKEAjw1MSvBRDj2IyP-
o7PygsSJAC_6zodh7pdBpD8cqKO15c9wDpsa0pgsIWf3zjHzt34mhh4wRoCNEbw_wcB

https://en.wikipedia.org/wiki/Cincinnati_and_Whitewater_Canal_Tunnel

Dearborn County Fair

Source - Dearborn County Fair Timeline by Liz Biersdorfer

July 6 - 31 1883 Lawrenceburg Register

1894 Chicago Times Article

From the July 18, 1935 Dearborn County Register

Dearborn Historical Marker St. John

http://www.ingenweb.org/infranklin/pages/tier2/immigration1.html

History of Dearborn County, Indiana: Her People, Industries and Institutions

https://books.google.com/books?id=c080AQAAMAAJ&pg=PA404&lpg=PA404&dq=st+j ohn+church+dover+indiana+1820&source=bl&ots=A5dwHsZqgz&sig=DKELWjpCdWbkk Vv74UnZV7KVhuY&hl=en&sa=X&ved=0ahUKEwi1lf6jyK3PAhUM2SYKHbVWCWoQ6A EIPDAF#v=onepage&q=st%20john%20church%20dover%20indiana%201820&f=false

http://www.hmdb.org/marker.asp?marker=86237

General John Morgan Dearborn County Historical Marker

http://www.hmdb.org/marker.asp?marker=86241

Dearborn County Historical Marker - General John Morgan

Indiana (Dearborn County), Dover — General John Morgan

Marched east along this road on Monday, July 13, 1863 in his raid across Southern Indiana. — Map (db m86241) HM

Dearborn Historical Marker - Abraham Lincoln

http://www.smithsonianmag.com/history/lincolns-whistle-stop-trip-to-washington-161974/?no-ist

http://www.historyplace.com/lincoln/

http://www.hmdb.org/marker.asp?marker=20600

Dearborn County Historical Marker - Lawrenceburg - Founded 1802

https://en.wikipedia.org/wiki/Albert_G._Porter

http://www.nga.org/cms/home/governors/past-governors-bios/page_indiana/col2-content/main-content-list/title_porter_albert.default.html

http://www.in.gov/history/2732.htm

http://www.in.gov/history/2727.htm

https://en.wikipedia.org/wiki/Winfield_T._Durbin

http://www.nga.org/cms/home/governors/past-governors-bios/page_indiana/col2-content/main-content-list/title_durbin_winfield.default.html

https://www.in.gov/history/files/inspanishamerwar.pdf

http://www.hmdb.org/marker.asp?marker=66907

Dearborn County Underground Railroad

http://www.rootsweb.ancestry.com/~indbchs/elijah.html

http://freedomcenter.org/freedom-forum/index.php/2010/07/dearborn-county-indiana/

http://freedomcenter.org/freedom-forum/index.php/2010/07/methodist-protestant-church-guilford-indiana/

http://www.undergroundrailroadindiana.com/

http://www.pbs.org/black-culture/shows/list/underground-railroad/stories-freedom/underground-railroad-terminology/

About the Author

Paul considers himself a bit of an Indiana hound, in that he likes to sniff out the interesting places and history of Indiana and use his books to tell people about them.

Join Paul on Facebook
https://www.facebook.com/Mossy-Feet-Books-474924602565571/
Twitter
https://twitter.com/MossyFeetBooks
mossyfeetbooks@gmail.com

Mossy Feet Books Catalog

To Get Your Free Copy of the Mossy Feet Books Catalogue, Click This Link.

http://mossyfeetbooks.blogspot.com/

Gardening Books

Fantasy Books

Humor

Science Fiction

Semi – Autobiographical Books

Travel Books

Sample Chapter
Indiana's Timeless Tales - Pre-History to 1781
Paul R. Wonning

Illinoisan Glacier Boundary

Visitors to Washington County on south central Indiana will find this marker placed by the Indiana Historical Bureau.

Title of Marker:

Illinoisan Glacier Boundary

Location:

NE corner of SR 135 & Lick Skillet Road, 8 miles north of Salem (Washington County, Indiana)

Installed by:

Erected 1995 Indiana Historical Bureau

Marker ID #:

88.1995.1

Marker Text:

Nearby is the boundary of the Illinoisan Glacier, which covered all but approximately 6,250 square miles in south, central area of Indiana. Most of Indiana's topography was affected by four separate glacial advancements during Pleistocene epoch, circa one million years ago.

Brief History By the Author:

Pleistocene Era

The Pleistocene Age began roughly two million years ago and ended about 10,000 years ago. During this vast period, at least three episodes of extensive glaciations covered most of what is now Indiana. These glacial events are called the Pre-Illinoisan, Illinoisan, and the Wisconsinan Ages.

The Ice Ages

The Pre-Illinoisan began about 1,200,000 years ago and ended about 550,000 years ago. An interglacial period followed that lasted several thousand years. The Illinoisan began approximately 350,000 years ago and lasted about 50,000 years. Another interglacial period followed this glacial event, followed by the last glacial period, the Wisconsin, which began about 150,000 years ago and ended approximately 10,000 to 12,000 years ago. A period of global warming has produced the climate we know today.

Different Landscapes

These glaciers created two vastly different landscapes in Indiana. The northern two thirds comprise what geologists call the Tipton Till. Glaciers covered this area during all four glacial events. The glaciers probably never touched the southern third. A hilly, heavily forested land still bears the marks of the vast water runoff that occurred when the Ice Age finally ended around 10,000 to 12,000 years ago. If the glaciers had never formed, all of Indiana would probably look like the southern third of the state.

The Glaciers Form

The Huron-Erie Lobe is the glacier that covered Indiana during the last glacial event. Scientists estimate that the average temperature of the earth was about six to twelve degrees Celsius colder than it is now. Sometime about two million years ago, Earth's climate cooled. Over vast regions of what is now Canada and North America the temperature dropped below freezing and remained there thorough the year. Snow fell and did not melt. More layers of snow covered this un-melted snow, building up layer after layer of snow. This weight of the accumulated snow turned the snow to ice. The ice formed layers up to two miles thick in the Great Lakes region. Over central Indiana, the glaciers were probably a mile thick. This gradually diminished as the ice reached its margins.

Flowing Ice

The pressure deep in the ice field caused the ice to become almost fluid in its movements. The ice flowed over the landscape, carving out rivers and lakes. It also created hills and the dune area around Lake Michigan. The weight of the ice sheet created the Great Lakes basin, and then filled that basin with melt water when the temperatures warmed and the ice melted. Geologist estimate that the ice moved about a foot a day, first advancing, and then retreating. Always grinding the terrain beneath it and changing it.

Southern Indiana

Most of the southern portion of the state had glaciers at different times; however, there is a segment in the south central region that has never, as far as scientists can tell, ever had glaciers. During the last episode, the boundary was a ragged line from approximately Terre Haute in the West to Brookville in the east. Below that, the older Karst topography of caves, sinkholes, knobs and disappearing steams that are not found in the northern areas

Indiana Geology

The glaciers' presence created the two basic landscapes we find today in Indiana. The northern two thirds of the state that the glaciers covered consists of a flat landscape that geologist refer to as the Tipton Till Plain, covering the bedrock. As the glaciers advanced and retreated over the eons, they carried dirt, rocks and other debris with them. When the last glaciers melted, they dropped this dirt and rock mixture right where they were. Geologists refer to four basic types of deposits left by the glaciers as till, outwash, Lacustrine and Silt.

The Four Types

Sand, silt, and clay combine with gravel and boulders are the main components fo glacial till. Till was deposited directly by the glacier and has remained largely in the same location. As the glaciers melted, the melt water formed layers of outwash. Heavier components like gravel and rock were deposited first. The silt, sand and clay particles were carried greater distances by the flowing melt water. The glaciers had carved out depressions in the landscape, which formed the many lakes found in northern Indiana. The silts deposited at the bottoms of these lakes are called Lacustrine. Winds carried the finer materials, called silt, and deposited them further away. These silt layers, called loess, were blown mostly from the Wabash and White River valleys. Near the river valleys, this loess sometimes formed thick layers.

Southern Indiana

Glaciers have never covered the southern one third of the state, as far as geologists can tell. This region has some of Indiana's most ancient soils and terrain. Most of the state's bedrock layer consists of limestone, dolostone, sandstone, and shale. Much of southern Indiana is under laid with limestone. Much of the southern area consists of Karst landscape. In this type of landscape acidic groundwater flows through the limestone bedrock, dissolving it. This action over time creates sinkholes in the surface, underground caverns and disappearing streams. One predominant feature of south central Indiana is the Knobstone Escarpment

Knobstone Escarpment

Geologists call the knobs the Knobstone Escarpment. They include some of Indiana's most rugged terrain. It stretches from Brown County State Park in the north to the Ohio River. Elevations range from 360 feet near the mouth of the Wabash River to Weed Patch Hill, which has an elevation of

1,056 feet above sea level. This hill is in Brown County State Park and is the third highest area in Indiana.

Limestone

Much of the limestone that Indiana is famous for is also found in the southern part of the state. Indiana's limestone deposits formed during the Ordovician period, about 1.5 million years ago when the land that is now Indiana lay near the tropics, covered with a warm, shallow sea. This sea was rich with marine organisms, such as brachiopods, bryozoans, trilobites, and corals. These organisms died and settled on the bottom of this sea. Through Continental drift, this land migrated north and around 40 million years ago, this sea dried up. Geologic forces lifted the land mass out of the sea. The limestone deposits became covered with sediment over the ages. Glaciers scoured the countryside during the Ice Age, exposing some of this rock.

Oolitic Limestone

Oolitic Limestone is made up of particles called ooliths. These small, carbonate particles are composed of concentric rings of calcium carbonate. Sand or shell fragments rolled around on the floor of this warm, shallow sea collecting a layer of limestone. The rocks consistent structure allows it to be easily sculpted or carved. The stone is almost perfect building material.

The Quarries of Indiana

Indiana's quarries produce rock known by many names, Indiana Limestone, Indiana Oolitic Limestone, Bedford Oolitic Limestone, and Bedford Rock. The limestone belt that produces this high quality stone encompasses most of Monroe and Lawrence Counties. Limestone of lesser quality underlies much of the rest of central and east central Indiana. Hoosiers began quarrying limestone during the middle of the Eighteenth Century. Indiana has been at the forefront of limestone production. Limestone from Indiana has been the preferred building material for many buildings from New York to Washington DC and other places. The Empire State Building has Indiana limestone as a major component of its structure.

Mossy Feet Books
www.mossyfeetbooks.com

Made in the USA
Middletown, DE
29 July 2023